# THE MINIMALIST MARRIAGE

How to Have Less Drama and
More Happiness in Your Relationship

Debra Macleod, B.A., LL.B.

© Debra Macleod   2018

ISBN-13: 978-1722224899

All rights reserved. No part of this publication may be reproduced, stored in a retrieval system, or transmitted in any form or by any means, electronic, mechanical, photocopying, recording or otherwise, without the prior written permission of the author.

Debra Macleod asserts the moral right to be identified as the author of this work. DebraMacleod.com

The author is not engaged in rendering professional advice or services to the individual reader. The relationship strategies presented herein are for general informational purposes and are based on the principles of effective communication, conflict resolution and positive interactions within marriage: they may not be suitable for all or serious marital problems. The author is not a mental health practitioner and this book is not appropriate in situations of mental illness or instability, or physical, sexual or emotional abuse of a spouse or child. Only the reader can judge the suitability of this book's content to his /her specific situation. The author will not be held liable for any act or omission allegedly arising, directly or indirectly, from the use or misuse of this book. All people, correspondence, and situations presented in this book have been fictionalized, altered and/or generalized for illustration purposes: names, dialogue and identifying details do not represent actual persons and any resemblance to actual persons is coincidental.

Cover Illustration:

Red velvet box heart. © Bulltus_casso. Provided by Shutterstock.com

Cover design by Rita Toews

Inside illustrations:

Continuous line. Electric light bulb. © Valenty. Provided by Shutterstock.com

*Praise for the Author*

"This book can kick-start a wreck of a relationship back into high gear." SUE JOHANSON, OXYGEN MEDIA

"For a sagging relationship, you can get the spark back again if the book's instructions are followed." THE WASHINGTON POST

"Most people spend the largest part of their adulthood slogging through committed relationships, and they need books like this." LIBRARY JOURNAL

"Deb's advice is like that wise but slightly mouthy aunt you go to when you need somebody to kick you in the pants and give you a hug at the same time." – CORUS MEDIA

"Informed, engaging and unapologetically good at what she does. Deb's our fave." – CITY TV

# TABLE OF CONTENTS

| | |
|---|---|
| Welcome | Page 7 |
| Bright Idea #1 | Page 11 |
| Bright Idea #2 | Page 14 |
| Bright Idea #3 | Page 16 |
| Bright Idea #4 | Page 18 |
| Bright Idea #5 | Page 20 |
| Bright Idea #6 | Page 22 |
| Bright Idea #7 | Page 23 |
| Bright Idea #8 | Page 25 |
| Bright Idea #9 | Page 30 |
| Bright Idea #10 | Page 32 |
| Bright Idea #11 | Page 34 |
| Bright Idea #12 | Page 35 |
| Bright Idea #13 | Page 44 |
| Bright Idea #14 | Page 46 |
| Bright Idea #15 | Page 48 |
| Bright Idea #16 | Page 50 |
| Bright Idea #17 | Page 52 |
| Bright Idea #18 | Page 55 |
| Bright Idea #19 | Page 56 |
| Bright Idea #20 | Page 57 |

| | |
|---|---|
| Bright Idea #21 | Page 63 |
| Bright Idea #22 | Page 65 |
| Bright Idea #23 | Page 67 |
| Bright Idea #24 | Page 68 |
| Bright Idea #25 | Page 70 |
| Bright Idea #26 | Page 74 |
| Bright Idea #27 | Page 76 |
| Bright Idea #28 | Page 78 |
| Bright Idea #29 | Page 80 |
| Bright Idea #30 | Page 81 |
| Bright Idea #31 | Page 83 |
| Bright Idea #32 | Page 86 |
| Bright Idea #33 | Page 90 |
| Bright Idea #34 | Page 93 |
| Bright Idea #35 | Page 94 |
| Bright Idea #36 | Page 97 |
| Bright Idea #37 | Page 99 |
| Bright Idea #38 | Page 100 |
| Bright Idea #39 | Page 102 |
| Bright Idea #40 | Page 105 |
| Bright Idea #41 | Page 107 |
| Bright Idea #42 | Page 109 |
| Bright Idea #43 | Page 111 |
| Bright Idea #44 | Page 113 |
| Bright Idea #45 | Page 116 |

Bright Idea #46                  Page 118

Bright Idea #47                  Page 120

Bright Idea #48                  Page 123

Bright Idea #49                  Page 125

Bright Idea #50                  Page 127

Goodbye                       Page 180

# WELCOME

In case you haven't noticed, there is a quiet but exciting revolution happening in our society. Many people have had enough of having too much and are consciously, even courageously, choosing a more minimalist lifestyle. They are learning to distinguish between what they need and what they need to get rid of. And they are finding profound freedom in that. They are also finding more time, more money and more peace of mind.

It's the same thing with married life. When you learn what to cling to and what to let go of, married life is simpler. When you learn how to interact with your spouse, how to prevent and respond to conflict, and when you learn how to do those things in the simplest terms possible, married life is happier. When you work together to clear the clutter – physical, emotional and mental – you're left with just the good stuff. That's what a minimalist marriage is all about.

So if you've ever stood back after cleaning out your closet or garage and thought *"Wow, I feel better,"* and you'd love to feel that same sense of streamlined simplicity and accomplishment in your married life, this little book is for you. In the spirit of minimalism, it isn't a page longer than it needs to be.

That's why you won't find drawn-out chapters here. Instead, you'll find a stream of practical strategies – bright ideas – that you can use starting right now. These are the bare minimums – the keepers! – in the cleaned-out closet of your marriage.

If you can master these basics, if you can live them day in and day out, you'll have a minimalist marriage that works. They aren't presented in any particular order; however, they are numbered so you can easily revisit the ones that most resonate with you.

**I want this little book to start a big revolution.**

A revolution against the patronizing, indulgent and theory-burdened marriage-saving business. Against labeling every marital interaction, dynamic or conflict as a syndrome or disorder, or making up a cutesy pop-culture term to describe it. Against blaming our childhood, our spouse, our job, whatever, for our own shortcomings or the problems in our marriage.

Against the magical "3 (or 7 or 10) steps to save your marriage" that someone has made up and that you don't get access to until you sign-up for the newsletter. Against trading in our own accountability, decision-making, personal judgment or preferences for someone else's opinion or advice.

Against making an excuse instead of doing some soul-searching and acting in the ways that we know, deep down, are right and mature and decent.

Against spending our hard-earned money, valuable time and precious energy on things that make other people rich and happy, while filling our own marriage with debt and drama.

And so on.

You've heard it said that "marriage is hard." That is a lie. Rocket science is hard. Marriage is, or at least should be, easy. Easygoing. Simple. The best things in life are simple.

But for your marriage to truly be simple, you need to strip away the excess. You need to minimize the distractions, complexities and superfluousness that vie for space in your relationship, regardless of where they come from.

Yet nowadays, that's easier said than done. Our society and culture are supersaturated with every form of excessiveness.

The pursuit of more – more stuff, more success, more money, more tech, more excitement, more sex, more validation, more reassurance, more solutions, more perfection…it's exhausting. It sucks the life out of, well, a life. It sucks the life out of a marriage, too.

Because it all leads to drama.

I see a lot of relationship drama in my private practice as a marriage conflict specialist. Emotional and sexual affairs, inappropriate friendships, self-indulgent midlife crises, chronic arguing and even pure apathy and indifference.

I see conflict in every shape and form. Conflict between spouses, with the in-laws, with the kids or step-kids, with the ex, with the bank.

My goal in this book isn't to oversimply these or other types of marriage problems. It isn't to offer a "one size fits all" cure. Rather, my goal here is to help you *minimize the chances* that your marriage will fall into conflict and drama. An ounce of prevention is worth a pound of cure.

Yet if your marriage is presently struggling with conflict or drama, don't panic. This book can complement the work you're doing in a larger sense to get back on track. Things may be complicated right now, but the goal should always be simplicity. You can get there.

In *The Minimalist Marriage,* I want to help you recognize what is essential and what is excessive. And I'm not just talking about physical things like cars or clothes. I'm talking about emotional, mental, behavioral and even spiritual things.

What is essential to a marriage's success? What is essential to keep and what is essential to do away with? Those are the simple questions we'll be answering here.

If you're familiar with the previous books or programs in my Marriage SOS series, you may recognize some (not all) of these strategies. If you aren't familiar with my previous work, you're going to love these no-nonsense insights and ideas.

All right. It's time to simplify and downsize. To minimize the excesses, distractions and complexities that cause unnecessary problems in marriage and life. To trash what doesn't work and treasure what does work.

**A minimalist marriage is a reliable way to experience less drama and more happiness in your relationship and in your life.**

Yet a minimalist marriage does ask something of you – change. It asks you to change, or at least challenge, the way you've been doing things to this point. And as we all know, change can be hard. Some people resist it. Some are downright defensive when it comes to facing it.

So as you read, I'll ask only one thing of you: keep an open mind. A minimalist marriage does fly in the face of many ideas, opinions and relationship habits that have become entrenched and expected in our society. Your knee-jerk reaction may be to say, "No way! I'm not doing that! I'm not giving that up!" You might even feel offended or indignant.

That's okay. You don't have to do anything you don't want to do and there may be concepts or suggestions that simply don't apply to your situation. But if you've read this far, you are searching for something. I hope you will keep reading to see whether you can find it here.

Good luck!

## Bright Idea #1

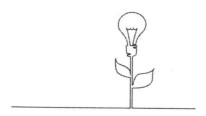

I just did a little experiment. I did a Google search for "how to have better work-life balance." There were 652, 000, 000 results. If a subject ever needed a minimalist approach, it's this one.

There are a few prevailing reasons why people struggle to have a healthy work-life balance. One common reason is because they're in so much debt that they're living hand to mouth and are in survival mode. It's hard to come home from work early and relax if you're worried you're about to lose your home.

This is of course one reason why minimalist marriages are so popular. Lose the financial pressure and sheer panic that comes from buying too much "stuff" and life is so much more livable!

Couples in a minimalist marriage make a conscious choice to rid themselves of excessive clutter, both in terms of physical items and marital conflict. They make a choice to reject the materialism of our society and the marketing culture that makes us believe, falsely believe, that we need more stuff – expensive stuff – to be successful. We are constantly made to feel that we must live up to some artificial, advertising-driven ideal of success.

A perfect example of this is the so-called "starter home." The name itself implies that it isn't quite good enough. You need a bigger house, a more expensive house. Yet when we stop to think about this, to challenge this, we realize that we don't need a bigger house. Who says we do? Your realtor. He wants his commission.

Other major industries from automotive to technology do the same thing.  We are constantly being pressured to trade in our paid-for vehicle and buy the newer, more expensive model…for which we of course need to take out another loan, with interest.

Think of the last time Apple or Samsung came out with their newest phone.  For some inexplicable reason, this makes worldwide headlines, right alongside news about this country's nuclear arsenal or that country's human rights violations.  It's just *that* important.

Except that it isn't.  **Couples in a minimalist marriage know consumerist bullshit when they see it and they're just not buying it anymore.**

Couples in a minimalist marriage don't want to work their asses off or delay retirement another five or ten years to pay a realtor's commission and yet another mortgage.

They don't want to stay late and miss out on events and good times to pay off that unnecessary high-interest loan for the new car they didn't need.  They don't want to delay a vacation to pay for some trendy phone that has one pointless extra feature than the previous one.  They don't want to work to make someone else rich.  They want to live their own life, not finance someone else's.

So if you're looking for a better work-life balance, this is my first bit of advice: take a critical look at what you are buying and why you're buying it.  Who really wants you to buy it?

There's a certain concept in the law called *cui bono*.  It's Latin for "who stands to benefit?"  We use this when we're trying to figure out who committed a crime.

*Oh, this elderly rich woman just died under suspicious circumstances?  And her new husband just inherited her fortune?  Hmm.  Let's take a closer look, here…*

The next time you feel a twinge of unworthiness because you have a starter-home, ask yourself: "Who stands to benefit if I buy a bigger house?"  Your realtor.  Your bank.  Not you.

The next time you feel tempted to reach into your wallet because your car is five years old or you don't have the new headline-making phone, ask yourself: "Who stands to benefit if I buy these things?" The car dealership. The tech company. Not you.

Another common reason that people can't achieve that peaceful work-life balance is because they're in the "rat race" mentality. Some people truly love that lifestyle and want it – and that's great. Know thyself. But other people find they're in a race they don't remember signing up for.

If you suspect that you fall into the latter category, I want you to do the same thing: take a critical look at why you're running the race and then ask yourself: "What do I get if I win this race? Is the prize worth the effort? Will it really make me happier or more fulfilled?

It's remarkable how simply slowing down and taking a more critical look at our lifestyle – our working and spending habits – can make us realize just how much we've been snookered.

Having a better work-life balance is simple. You don't need to sift through millions of search results. You just need to do two things. First, stop buying stuff you don't need. Second, stop running a race you don't even care about winning.

## BRIGHT IDEA #2

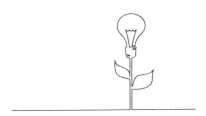

Okay, this is a touchy subject so we're going to tackle it early on. In the interests of having a minimalist and drama-free marriage, I suggest you **limit or restrict any potentially problematic opposite-sex friendships** you have in your marriage.

But what is a potentially problematic opposite-sex friendship? At its basic, it's one that involves two people who, if circumstances were different (i.e. one or both weren't married), could be potential sexual partners. There may be an underlying current of attraction between them, especially if they are similar in age or attributes.

There's no doubt that the messiest, most destructive and dramatic problem that can strike a marriage is some form of infidelity. And in my practice, the vast majority of affairs that I see began as opposite-sex friendships.

These begin innocently enough but soon start to take more time and energy away from the marriage. Spouses begin to argue about this and, all the while, the "friendship" grows in intensity and intimacy until the befriending spouse is more protective of the friendship than their own marriage.

Our society sends the message that the more friendships we have, the happier we will be. That isn't always true. In fact, a person with even one high-quality friendship will be much happier than a person with a thousand low-quality friends on social media.

Not all friendships are created equal. And that's certainly true when it comes to opposite-sex friendships within marriage.

If you want to cut down on the type of clutter than can potentially bury a marriage in heartache, divided loyalties, anxiety and ultimately betrayal, you'll ignore the false social message that opposite-sex friendships within marriage are harmless.

Remember that marriage is made for two. Adding that third person – that overly intimate opposite-sex friend – doesn't just take up too much time and space in our already busy lives, it has the potential to drive a serious wedge between otherwise loving spouses.

And who has time for that kind of drama?

# BRIGHT IDEA #3

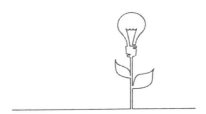

It often happens that a spouse brings unnecessary drama into their marriage by acquiring relationship advice from either too many different sources or from the wrong sources.

I've had clients come to me after seeing multiple counselors or coaches, talking to friends and family members, even seeking the advice of an astrologer, pastor or other spiritual advisor. Some have spent weeks on online comment boards, asking total strangers to chime in on their marriage issues: *Do you think my spouse is cheating on me? Is it wrong for my spouse to talk to this other woman/man?*

It's true that there's wisdom in the counsel of many. It's equally true that you must **trust your own interpretation of events**.

Let's consider the above question: *Is it wrong for my spouse to talk to this other woman/man?* The advice a worried spouse receives will depend on the person giving it. On that person's experiences or biases, or their training, personality or agenda.

That means that each person is likely going to offer a different piece of advice. That advice is going to pile up to complicate and cloud the issue.

A counselor or coach may say that you need to trust your spouse and respect their opposite-sex friendships. A pastor may say that you need to pray about it. A bitter divorced friend may say that your spouse is definitely cheating.

And the more you listen to each of these people, the more they try to convince you (consciously or not) that they're right about what's happening, the more confused you will become. The more you will reach out to even more people for even more advice, and the less you will listen to your own little voice and trust your own instincts. All the while, the drama builds in your marriage.

That's why **self-reliance is essential in a minimalist marriage**. Learn to trust your own assessment of a situation and listen to your own little voice. After all, you know your marriage and your spouse best. If you truly feel that your spouse is spending too much time or energy on another person (for example), then go with that feeling and talk to your spouse about it.

Your interpretation, your assessment, of what is happening in your own marriage is more valid than anyone else's. That one little voice – yours – is worth more than a chorus of others.

## BRIGHT IDEA #4

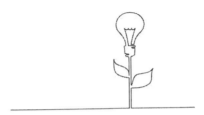

My husband and I have a son who's good at a lot of things. Like most kids his age, he's especially good at one thing – trying to divide and conquer his parents so that he can get his own way.

For example, he might ask his dad if he can have a certain video game. If his dad says no because he didn't do his chores, he'll move on to ask me; however, he won't tell me that his dad said no. What he will do is tell me about the fantastic grade he just got on the science test. Then he'll ask for the video game. And if, dazzled by his A+, I say yes, then it's mission accomplished for him.

Of course, this then leads to my husband asking me, "Why did you let him buy the game? I already said no." And while he and I are in the kitchen trying to figure out what just happened, our son is in the basement gleefully blasting aliens.

If you have kids, this is probably a familiar scenario to you. And you've probably found yourself falling into arguments where you're trying to figure out who promised what and when, and maybe even arguing with your spouse about why they said yes or no.

Well, here's an easy way to avoid the drama. **Have a united front with your spouse at all times.** Even if you don't agree with something your spouse has done, don't question them until you're behind closed doors. Let everyone – your kids, family, friends – see you as a united front, as a couple who always and unquestioningly backs each other up.

This doesn't mean you won't disagree with your spouse. It just means that you won't let other people see you disagree. And that's important for a number of reasons.

**By having a united front, you keep things simple and predictable.** Your kids learn that they can't divide and conquer you. Eventually, they'll stop trying. It just isn't worth the effort. As a result, you'll reduce those "but Mom said I could!" arguments.

You'll also reduce the kinds of arguments that we often see with in-laws. For example, take the case of a pushy mother-in-law (I know, it's a stereotype, but stick with me). She wants to have her son over for Easter supper, so she phones him directly – strategically avoiding her daughter-in-law – and pressures him into coming.

If he gives in without first checking with his wife, the fight is on at home. His wife feels sidelined and resentful. She feels that his mother has more influence in his life than she does. That's going to create drama in their marriage. A lot of drama.

However, if the mother-in-law knows from experience that her son is going to insist on checking with his wife first, before committing to spending Easter supper at his mom's house, this mother-in-law is more likely to respect this couple's marriage. She is more likely to develop a rapport with her daughter-in-law and even call her first.

And that is going to avoid a lot of drama as the years go by.

A wonderful thing about minimalist marriages is that the "rules" are clear not just to the husband and wife, but to everyone else who knows and interacts with the couple: kids, in-laws, extended family, friends, neighbors and so on. This keeps things simple.

## BRIGHT IDEA #5

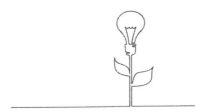

You'll recall that in the welcome message to this book I asked you to keep an open mind. I gave you the heads-up that you might be asked to challenge some of the ways you live and the ways that society expects all of us to live. You already did that to some extent when I asked you to reconsider having opposite-sex friendships in your marriage (see bright idea #2).

Well, this is a similar challenge. So take a deep breath and hear me out. Here, I recommend that you **delete your social media accounts**. All of them. Yes, you read that right.

Social media accounts are not necessary for life. They are not necessary to maintain friendships or connections. If they are, those friendships or connections are likely not that significant.

I have seen, time and time again, that couples who are very active on social media have marriages that are "cluttered" in so many ways.

Their perception of what's important, what's real, becomes skewed. They often become more concerned with impressing others than living in the moment.

They become addicted to checking in with what's happening, terrified that they're missing something. They feel compelled to share everything from their vacations to their dinner plates with the world – a world which, don't fool yourself, couldn't care less.

In the worst cases, spouses begin to have suspicions or insecurities about who their partner is talking to via social media. It's all too easy for an old flame or new co-worker to reach out. It's almost like they know when a marriage is at a low point and they choose that time to swoop in. I've called these folks "partner predators" and that's exactly what they are.

And once they're on the prowl, you can expect the drama in your marriage to ramp up like never before.

Yet despite both the potential and proven problems that social media can cause in a marriage, people are often shocked when I suggest they delete their social media accounts. Some act as if the request is impossible. They may respond with defensiveness, panic or incredulousness.

Ask yourself: why is that? The answer is this: because social media is painstakingly designed to keep us coming back for more and to make us feel as though we're missing something if we don't.

Every time you hit that "refresh" button looking for the newest post, you're a lab rat pushing down on a lever looking for a treat.

Remember that a minimalist marriage isn't just about reducing our physical belongings. **A minimalist marriage is about liberating ourselves – body, mind and spirit – from the things that litter our lives, waste our time and complicate our marriage.**

Social media has the potential to do all of those things in abundance. Whatever payoff you get from it in terms of convenience, whatever momentary feeling of being connected or validated you get, it just isn't worth the cost or the risk to your marriage.

I promise, you will not die if you delete your social media accounts. You may, however, rediscover your life.

# BRIGHT IDEA #6

Sometimes we're at a loss for words and don't know what to say to our spouse. Perhaps we're upset or irritated with them. Maybe we're in a sour mood or feeling stressed. Or maybe we're just busy and their call came at an inconvenient time.

At a moment like that, it can be all too easy to snap at our spouse or to speak to them in a critical, dismissive or harsh way, thereby making the situation even worse. That complicates what should've simply been a passing moment and leads to unnecessary, often escalating drama.

No matter what words you use to say "I'm mad at you" or "I'm in a bad mood" or "I can't talk right now," just remember to keep one thing consistent – and that's your tone of voice. **Make sure your voice tone always conveys a sense of respect and affection for your spouse.** Always be aware of your voice tone and get into the habit of controlling it, regardless of what's happening.

I've heard many spouses say of their partner, "It's not *what* they say, it's *how* they say it."

The tone of voice you use has an incredible ability to affect how your partner feels and responds to you, and in turn, how the rest of your interaction is going to proceed.

Voice tone is also contagious. Use an unpleasant one, and that's what you'll get back. Use a pleasant one – better, a loving one – and that's what you're likely to hear back from your spouse.

## BRIGHT IDEA #7

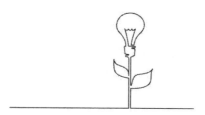

If the minimalist marriage were to have one prevailing maxim, it would be this – **always put your spouse first.**

Yet that's not the message we tend to hear, is it? More often than not, we're asked to think about whether our marriage is working for us, whether we're happy, whether we're having our needs met. The initial focus is on our happiness, *not* our partner's.

I remember consulting with a certain client whose marriage had been a miserable one for years. It was our first session and I was just running through a few questions when she stopped me in mid-sentence to pass me a list.

It was a list she had given her husband a few days prior, and it was titled, "20 Things I Need From You Starting Today."

It's not the first time I've seen a client do this type of thing. A few other notable lists I've seen were titled, "The Top 10 Things You're Doing Wrong," "17 Reasons I'm Leaving You," and "6 Things *My* Therapist Said *You* Should Do Every Day."

This approach is doomed. The truth is, you cannot reasonably expect someone to prioritize your happiness when you haven't bothered to prioritize theirs. That's just how people are.

Worse, when you put your own happiness before your partner's, you establish a nasty dynamic where your partner also puts their happiness before yours.

A successful minimalist marriage has the exact *opposite* dynamic. In it, both spouses are doing their very best to put each other's happiness before their own.

And that's the dynamic that every marriage, especially the minimalist marriage, should strive for. It leads to a highly functional, collaborative marriage where both spouses are considerate of each other's lives, needs, preferences and happiness.

In such marriages, spouses have a "default approach" where they automatically consider their spouse first, whether it's during day to day interactions or when making a decision. *How will this impact my spouse? Will this make my spouse's life easier or happier? How will my spouse feel about this or react to this?*

Taking those few seconds to consider these kinds of questions is, without a doubt, the most reliable way to **prevent relationship conflict** from happening in the first place. It's also a fantastic way to gain a deeper understanding of each other.

If you're not there yet, lead the way! Start putting your spouse first. They'll notice and, with some luck, will start doing the same. That's because "like attracts like" in marriage. If you treat your spouse well, they will be far more likely to return the favor.

**Don't make it more complicated than this.** In most marriages, it isn't necessary to study your interactions or classify your or your partner's personality types. Put each other first. Learn about each other in a natural way. That's a hallmark of a minimalist marriage.

Consider the client I just talked about. Imagine that instead of giving her husband such an obnoxious and self-focused list, she would have instead handed him a list titled, "20 Things I Can Do To Make You Happier."

How do you think her husband might have received that? We can't know for sure, but if I were in Vegas, I'd bet he would have received that with a heart full of love, gratitude and a renewed commitment to make his wife as happy as possible.

## BRIGHT IDEA #8

Putting your spouse first (see bright idea #7) is an effective minimalist approach to prevent relationship conflict from taking root in your marriage. Yet as all married couples know, conflict of some kind is unavoidable. So how do you handle it when it happens?

Some couples choose to go to marriage counseling. While this can work, it doesn't have a stellar success rate. Between the overdiagnosis of disorders or syndromes (which are then used as excuses), the individualist focus and the adversarial "Me vs. You" dynamic that can develop, couples counseling can add unhelpful clutter to conflict.

The same goes for many marriage self-help fad systems that rely on unproven or made-up psychological theories. These are often complex and cutesy in equal parts, usually suggesting that you classify your spouse as a "type" of some kind. Again, this can lead to more conflict, complications and clutter when you discover you just can't squeeze your spouse into a pigeonhole after all.

Yet before I can offer you an alternative and what I believe to be a more effective and minimalist way to resolve conflict, I have to give you a bit of background so it will make sense to you.

Many years ago, when dinosaurs roamed the Earth, I graduated from law school and started my own divorce mediation practice. That was how I began my career – helping people separate amicably.

As time went on, I noticed that many of my clients were getting divorced despite having gone to couples counseling or trying other forms of marriage help. Obviously these things weren't working as well as they should for many people.

That prompted me to shift the focus of my practice. Instead of helping couples separate, I adapted my skill set to offer an alternative to counseling, one that drew from my training in communication, law, mediation and conflict resolution.

I won't bore you with the particulars, but the bottom line is this: I encouraged spouses to see things from their partner's point of view instead of digging in their heels and only seeing things from their own point of view.

I encouraged them – at least for starters – to put their own emotions and assumptions on hold and to focus on understanding their spouse's position.

I assured them that they didn't have to agree with their spouse's position or forgive their spouse for anything. I simply wanted them to understand the other side of things in the same way that a lawyer understands the other side of things.

To do this, I would ask each spouse to **act as the other's advocate**. As their lawyer.

An example will best illustrate this. I'll use a recent almost-conflict that my husband and I experienced.

Not long before writing this book, I left on a business trip and was gone several days. When I returned home, my husband sheepishly admitted that he had made a large purchase without checking with me (see bright idea #30).

He had bought, sight unseen, a car from a Japanese online auto auction. He had done this once before, but that time we had done it together and the purchase price had been much lower. This time was an impulse and unilateral purchase and very out of character for him.

When he first told me about it, I resisted the urge to react out of anger or say something like, "Are you kidding me? You just spent thousands of dollars without telling me first?"

Instead, I took my own advice.

I put my own emotions and assumptions on hold for a few moments. I then did a simple mental exercise where I put myself in the role of his advocate, his lawyer. And I plead his case for him.

It went something like this:

*History:* In decades of marriage, Don has never made an impulse purchase, especially not a pricey one. This is the first time.

*Impact:* The purchase was pricey, but not worryingly so. We can afford it. It doesn't cause any financial problems.

*Intent:* To recapture and remember a happy family experience.

I'll elaborate on intent. We had recently returned home from a long trip to Italy. It was one of those fantastically fun trips where the things that went smoothly were wonderful and the things that didn't go smoothly were even more wonderful.

The particular experience that Don was reliving when he made the impulse purchase happened while we were driving on the Autostrada between Tivoli and Stabia. We were having a great time in the car, listening to music and trying to interpret Italian road signs when Don looked in his side-view mirror and said, "What the hell is that coming up behind us?"

We all turned to watch the strangest car we had ever seen pass us. After some in-car Googling, we learned it was a 2003 Fiat Multipla. Google it (including the year). It's weird. In fact, it has the distinction of having been crowned the world's ugliest car by many international automotive journalists.

Despite this, we fell in love with it. Not just the car, but the memory of it all and it became one of our favorite experiences during the trip.

You can probably guess what kind of car Don had imported.

As I ran through the mitigating factors of Don's purchase, I felt my anger dissolving and my affection growing.

And do you know what? This all happened in a matter of moments. We didn't have to complicate or clutter the issue with an irrelevant discussion about finances or unilateral decisions.

Instead of convicting him of some grievous marital offense, his sentence was a lot sweeter. And do you know what else? We love our Fiat Multipla.

Of course, conflict is complicated and if gets a lot messier and more hurtful than the situation I've outlined here. A partner's history can be more problematic. Their intent can be less noble and the impact on the marriage can be deeply harmful.

As a practitioner who specializes in higher-conflict issues like infidelity, I know this very well. My purpose here isn't to trivialize conflict or suggest that it can always be resolved in such a simple, minimalist way.

But it often – I would say *usually* – can be. **And that's what a minimalist marriage is all about. It's about resolving conflict in the simplest way possible so that unnecessary complexities don't add clutter.**

Often, all it takes to resolve conflict is for both spouses to act as each other's advocate.

Why? Because once you understand where another person is coming from, once you understand what they're feeling and thinking and what their true intention or motivation was, you are far less likely to see them as the enemy.

You realize they're not an adversary or someone to be beaten. They're not unlike you, they're not against you.

You realize that reconnection is possible and you learn to prioritize your partnership above all else.

While all of the concepts in this book are designed to prevent and resolve conflict – thereby reducing drama and increasing happiness – I recommend that you make a mental note of bright ideas #7, #8 and # 41.

These three concepts are of central importance in a minimalist marriage. When it comes to the task of preventing and resolving conflict in the simplest terms possible, they are key.

# BRIGHT IDEA #9

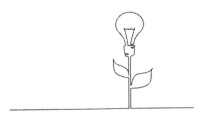

While I may not agree that "marriage is hard" (a good marriage shouldn't be hard!), I am willing to agree that one particular type of marriage can be hard – the second or subsequent marriage.

Yes, some of them are great. In the best of circumstances, spouses understand what made their previous marriage fail and they use that insight to enjoy a happier and more successful second or subsequent marriage.

If they have kids from a previous marriage, they work together, as a team, to create a blended family that works better for everyone than the previous living situation did.

Hats off to those folks. I admire you for making a positive change in your life. I hope having a minimalist marriage will make this relationship last.

Yet this bright idea is specifically for those couples who are still in their first marriage: **do your best to keep your first marriage intact.**

It may not be politically-correct to say so, but there is little doubt that a successful minimalist marriage will be easier to achieve with a first marriage. That's especially so if you have children.

Second and subsequent marriages often (not always) have more "stuff" in them. More history, more baggage, more negative experiences with relationships and so on.

If there are kids involved, there may be the extra drama that comes from custody battles, visitation schedules and child support payments. You may not be crazy about your new spouse's children and your new spouse may not be crazy about your kids. Your respective children may not get along. They may resent being thrust into a situation they have no control over and may act out.

There may be ongoing issues with everything from family planning to vacation planning. There may be residual issues with finances, property or assets, ex-in-laws and other extended family members or friend circles.

There may be lingering feelings between you and your ex-spouse as you begin to realize that the grass isn't always greener on the other side of the fence.

And that's it. Just a friendly reminder to treasure the relative simplicity of a first marriage.

## BRIGHT IDEA #10

In years gone by, couples who sought professional help tended to present with four main complaints – poor communication, sexual issues, money problems or an infidelity. These days, there's a fifth – their spouse's phone!

Personal technology – smartphones, tablets and a host of other gadgets – are never more than an arm's length away. Like social media, they are designed to be addictive and many of us can't go more than several minutes without checking our phone.

If it chimes or vibrates with some kind of message, we feel compelled to check it, regardless of where we are, what we're doing or who we're with. And if we happen to forget it (or the battery dies) we feel like we're missing an arm. We feel incomplete. We might even feel anxious or unsettled.

Obviously, phones and personal technology can be very convenient and useful. Unlike social media accounts (see bright idea #5) they are often a necessary part of modern life, one that lets us stay in touch with family and work. But that doesn't mean we can't take a few steps to limit the damage they can do to a marriage.

Because they can do a lot of damage. A spouse who constantly checks their phone, immediately responds to every unimportant text message, chronically surfs for trivial information or tunes out during a conversation to return a non-urgent email can make their partner feel both irritated and unimportant.

I don't think I've had a client consultation in the last decade where one partner didn't express a complaint along these lines. And these are just the minor problems!

In more serious cases, a partner's phone is the gateway to an emotional or physical affair. The vast majority of affairs begin as innocent friendships (see bright idea #2) that transition into intimate relationships. This transition is almost always facilitated by texting.

Texting creates a false sense of intimacy and connection between two people. It's all too easy to go from "hi" to "i miss u" to even more serious and sexual content. People say things via text that they would never say in person. It's low-risk. It's easy to hide. And that's why it's such a common way to start and sustain an affair.

If you want to have a truly minimalist (and successful) marriage, it is absolutely essential that you **cut down on how much you use your phone** and that you use it and other forms of personal technology with restraint, respect and discretion.

I have an easy three-step process to help you do this:

Step One – See your phone use from your partner's point of view. How does it impact them? What message does it send?
*(Excessive use of my phone makes my spouse feel unloved, unimportant and irritated. It sends the message that my phone, or whoever I'm texting, is more important and interesting than them.)*

Step Two - Distinguish between essential and non-essential use.
*(Responding to work calls/texts/email while on-call is essential. Responding to a call from our child's school is essential. Responding to a friend's text about her weekend is non-essential.)*

Step Three - Set rules and time-limits for non-essential use.
*(No phones in the bedroom. Leave phones in the car when you go to see a movie or watch your kid's school play. Don't spend more than 20 minutes a day in non-essential texting with friends.)*

# BRIGHT IDEA #11

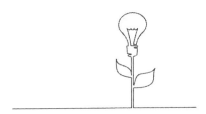

A minimalist marriage is about liberating ourselves – body, mind and spirit – from the things that clutter our lives, waste our time and complicate our marriage.

Part of that is **reducing our physical belongings**. Here are a few pointers to help you de-clutter your physical space:
- Get rid of things you don't need or haven't used in a year.
- Get rid of duplicate items.
- Get rid of things that don't serve a purpose.
- Resist the urge, that marketing ploy, to "upgrade" items or devices that are still perfectly functional.
- When you do need to make a new purchase, make sure it's a high-quality item so you won't need to replace it anytime soon.
- Love what you have and, if you've fallen out of love with it, try to rediscover it in some way (i.e. paint it).
- Digitize your movie or music collections.
- Only keep enough household items (i.e. cups, glasses, towels) that are necessary to serve the number of people in your household plus two guests.
- Eat meals made of similar ingredients so you're not throwing food out.
- For items with sentimental value (i.e. your kids artwork), choose one to five items that represent that "period" in your or your child's life and toss the rest. Don't feel guilty! It's good for you.

# BRIGHT IDEA #12

There's one very important thing that all minimalist marriages need to reduce – and when I say reduce, I actually mean rid themselves of altogether.

And that is debt. **You need to rid your marriage of debt.** You need to *completely* rid it of debt.

There are only a few things that really keep us up at night. Health worries, something going on with our kids…and money problems. And of those three things, money problems is probably the one that we can have the most power over. So use your power for good! Work together, as a couple, to get out of debt. You'll sleep easier.

You'll also have a better marriage, one that is less cluttered with all the marriage troubles that stem from money problems.

Have you ever seen that whack-a-mole game? Where one cute little rodent creature pops up and you try to whack it with a hammer only to have another one pop up in a different location?

Debt is like that. Money problems are like that. They create "pop up" problems in all areas of your marriage. They affect how you parent your kids. They affect your intimacy and sex life. They affect the way you feel and think about each other. They affect your health and sleep and well-being.

It all piles up.

Put your heads together and plan how to get out of debt. It doesn't haven't to happen quickly – it probably can't and won't happen quickly – but I promise, once you get started, you will feel a much greater sense of control and headway in your life.

There's an extra bonus, too. Couples who work together to get their spending and debt under control feel a profound sense of shared accomplishment. They feel like they can take on the world and overcome any problem, as long as they're together.

So instead of letting your debt divide you, why not let it bring you closer together?

Yet that's sometimes easier said than done. Finances can be intimidating and confusing. It can be hard to get organized and budget. Couples often talk about it, get motivated, but then drop the ball when it comes to actually doing it. And those kinds of perceived failures or disappointments add clutter to marriage.

That's why I've included the following guidelines and sample budget. This isn't exhaustive and you will have to amend it for your specific situation; however, it is enough to get you started and you can always consult a financial advisor if you need more advice or help (i.e. lowering interest rates, consolidating debt, etc.)

Here is a three-step process to help your minimalist marriage rid itself of debt:

1) Agree on a common financial goal for your future
2) Assess income vs. deductions, and
3) Create a balanced, realistic budget

1) *Agree on a common financial goal for your future*

This should include specific goals to pay off a mortgage or debt, as well as goals about vacationing, retirement, paying for a child's post-secondary education, etc.

_____

_____

_____

_____

_____

2) Assess income vs. deductions

This may include income (salary, tips, bonuses, pensions, etc.) and deductions (tax, pension plans, union dues, etc.).

## INCOME

_____     $_____

_____     $_____

_____     $_____

_____     $_____

## DEDUCTIONS

_____  $_____

_____  $_____

_____  $_____

_____  $_____

## Net Monthly Income

(income minus deductions)   $_____

3) Create a realistic budget

The budget framework and monthly expenses that follow under this heading are for example purposes only. They are not exhaustive and may not be applicable to your particular situation. Feel free to add things, remove things, amend things. Make it yours!

*A fool and his money are soon parted. I would pay anyone a lot of money to explain that to me.*

- Homer Simpson, *The Simpsons Television Show*

## **HOUSING**

| | | | |
|---|---|---|---|
| Mortgage / Rent | $_____ | Taxes | $_____ |
| Insurance | $_____ | Electricity | $_____ |
| Heat | $_____ | Water | $_____ |
| Telephone | $_____ | Cell Phone | $_____ |
| Internet | $_____ | Cable TV | $_____ |
| Home Repair | $_____ | Lawn Care | $_____ |
| Other | $_____ | Other | $_____ |

HOUSING SUBTOTAL          $_____


## **FOOD & HOUSEHOLD**

| | | | |
|---|---|---|---|
| Groceries | $_____ | Lunches | $_____ |
| Dining Out | $_____ | Cleaners | $_____ |
| Toiletries | $_____ | Laundry | $_____ |
| Hair Care | $_____ | Pets | $_____ |
| Other | $_____ | Other | $_____ |
| Other | $_____ | Other | $_____ |

FOOD & HOUSEHOLD
SUBTOTAL          $_____

## **CHILDCARE**

| | | | |
|---|---|---|---|
| Nanny | $_____ | Daycare | $_____ |
| Babysitter | $_____ | Other | $_____ |

CHILDCARE SUBTOTAL         $_____

## **CLOTHING**

| | | | |
|---|---|---|---|
| Children | $_____ | Self | $_____ |
| Spouse | $_____ | Other | $_____ |

CLOTHING SUBTOTAL         $_____

## **TRANSPORTATION**

| | | | |
|---|---|---|---|
| Car Loan(s) | $_____ | Insurance | $_____ |
| Registration | $_____ | Fuel / Oil | $_____ |
| Maintenance | $_____ | Parking | $_____ |
| Bus / Taxi | $_____ | Other | $_____ |

TRANSPORTATION SUBTOTAL         $_____

## **HEALTH & MEDICAL**

| | | | |
|---|---|---|---|
| Health Fees | $_____ | Insurance | $_____ |
| Dental | $_____ | Eye Care | $_____ |
| Prescriptions | $_____ | Massage | $_____ |
| Counselling | $_____ | Diet Needs | $_____ |
| Other | $_____ | Other | $_____ |

HEALTH & MEDICAL
SUBTOTAL                $_____


## **EDUCATION**

| | | | |
|---|---|---|---|
| School Fees | $_____ | Books | $_____ |
| Supplies | $_____ | Activities | $_____ |
| Other | $_____ | Other | $_____ |

EDUCATION
SUBTOTAL                $_____

## **RECREATION**

| | | | |
|---|---|---|---|
| Kids' Sports | $_____ | Lessons | $_____ |
| Books | $_____ | Movies | $_____ |
| Travel | $_____ | Club Fees | $_____ |
| Gifts | $_____ | Alcohol | $_____ |
| Other | $_____ | Other | $_____ |
| Other | $_____ | Other | $_____ |

RECREATION SUBTOTAL          $_____

## **MISCELLANEOUS**

| | | | |
|---|---|---|---|
| Donations | $_____ | Savings | $_____ |
| Life Insurance | $_____ | Other Tax | $_____ |
| Other | $_____ | Other | $_____ |

MISCELLANEOUSS
SUBTOTAL                     $_____

**TOTAL OVERALL EXPENSES**       $ _____

**TOTAL OVERALL INCOME**         $ _____

**OVERALL SURPLUS / SHORTFALL**  $ _____

## BRIGHT IDEA #13

A minimalist marriage thrives in a clutter-free environment. The more a couple reduces the excesses, complications and distractions that can cause problems, the more liberated they feel.

Almost everyone who subscribes to a minimalist marriage or lifestyle will tell you that their clutter-free environment has a profound impact on their emotional and mental well-being.

They feel more creative, more organized, more at peace, more productive, more in control. They feel happier.

Yet "clutter-free" has a little sister. And her name is cleanliness. **Keeping a clean home** can similarly make you feel better emotionally and mentally. And as you'll see, it can help your marriage avoid problems, too.

I've always been one of those people who has to clean my house before I do anything requiring any amount of focus. When I was in university, I couldn't study or start a paper until my apartment was squeaky clean.

Before I started this book I cleaned my house top to bottom. It's a physical action, but it's emotionally and mentally cleansing as well. It's like starting off with a clean slate.

If you're the type of person who felt drawn to this book and the subject of minimalism, you probably know exactly what I'm talking about.

So keep it going. When you clean your space, you clean your slate. You let your creativity, thoughts and feelings exist in a pure place.

And along with eliminating dirt, you'll eliminate a common marriage problem – arguments over cleanliness. I've had many couples in my office who were struggling with this.

I remember one particular couple who had managed to escalate their difference of opinion regarding cleanliness into an issue of competing values.

The wife admitted to being messy and not being too concerned about keeping a clean house. She said, "I have more important things to do, like spending time with my kids. I value my family more than a clean floor."

Her insinuation, of course, was that her husband's values were skewed because he wanted the house to be cleaner.

After working with this couple for a session (and focusing largely on the concepts you'll find in bright ideas #7, 8 and 41) they did become much more collaborative and respectful of each other's points of view and preferences.

Two more things to mention here before we move on.

First, be reasonable when it comes to cleanliness. It's no good to live in a filthy home; however, it's no fun to live in a show-home either! You don't need a sterile environment – nobody's doing surgery on your kitchen floor. Aim for neat and tidy.

Second, be sure to share house-cleaning duties or at least divide them up in a way that is fair and doable in light of your lifestyle. Don't be afraid to enlist the help of your kids, either. A toddler can learn to put his toys in a box and a teenager can learn how to do laundry. Let the little darlings earn their keep!

## BRIGHT IDEA #14

All right, I'm about to contradict myself here. Sort of. So far, and throughout this book, the goal is to have a minimalist marriage by reducing clutter and conflict, whether physical, emotional, mental or interpersonal.

Yet even a minimalist marriage can enjoy the sweet and thoughtful romantic gesture of gift-giving. In fact, I encourage it. The question becomes, what kind of gift do you give your spouse when you're both trying really hard to get rid of stuff?

Well, let me give you a guideline that might help. When deciding what kind of gift to give your spouse, try to make sure it meets one of these criteria. It can be:

A) used
B) consumed
C) experienced

I was recently working with a couple who was making the transition into a minimalist marriage when this gift-giving issue came up. They had always been the type of couple that exchanged spontaneous gifts and they didn't want to stop doing that.

We did some brainstorming and came up with the above criteria, and I think they did a brilliant job of making this work.

For example, the wife gifted her husband – an avid motorcyclist – with a very useful helmet. It had Bluetooth built into it so that he didn't have to worry about missing a work call during his fairly long commute home from the office. He loved it and it was something he used almost every single day.

When it was the husband's turn, he gifted his wife – a wine lover – with a "wine of the month" club. Every month she received a bottle of something delish from around the world, and she loved it. And yes, consumed it!

The next gift was bicycles. When their teenage son grew out of his bike, the husband bought his son a bigger one but also bought he and his wife bicycles at the same time. Neither of them had pushed a pedal since they were kids, but the purchase introduced a fun, new experience to their married life. Instead of taking evening walks together, they hopped on their bikes together.

I admit that gift-gifting can be tough and that's even more so in a minimalist marriage; however, I encourage you to slow down and put some thought into it. You know your spouse and lifestyle best, so challenge yourself to give gifts that can be used, consumed or experienced. There's no reason these can't be romantic.

## BRIGHT IDEA #15

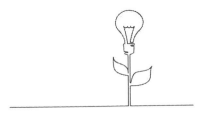

In my years of practice, I've worked with more couples than I can remember. I've encountered all kinds of personality traits, good and bad, and I've seen how these impact the quality of a marriage.

One of the worst personality traits that I see (and unfortunately I see it more all the time) is a lack of humility. This is the person who thinks just a little too highly of themselves and who basically believes that their spouse is lucky to be with them.

And wow, can this tear a marriage apart.

If you're going to have a minimalist marriage, there are a few personality traits that need to hit the dust bin as soon as possible – and a streak of narcissism is the first. Please, **have humility.**

Realize that while you may be a pretty awesome person, your spouse isn't lucky to have you. You're lucky to have each other.

Yet having humility isn't just admitting that you're not the world's most gorgeous / intelligent / wealthiest / interesting person.

It's also accepting that your way isn't the only way.

It's having the willingness to consider your partner's opinions or ideas on their own merit, not marginalizing them when they don't suit your purpose. Your spouse has their own needs, feelings, thoughts, beliefs and preferences. And all of them are just as valid as yours.

If both spouses can accept this about themselves, they will take a big step toward reducing needless conflict and having a marriage that lasts.

Because if narcissists don't change, the result is always the same. Their spouse will put up with them for a while, maybe until the kids are gone or there's enough money in the bank, and then they'll leave.

# BRIGHT IDEA #16

I was doing a live radio interview the other day when the show host asked me a question: "What is the number one complaint you hear from unhappy spouses?"

The answer came easily: "My spouse doesn't appreciate me."

It doesn't matter what the marriage problem is. It can be minor or major. It can be an emotional or physical affair, chronic arguing, even indifference or apathy.

Regardless of the problem, the most common complaint, the one that attends almost every marriage crisis, is feeling unappreciated by one's husband or wife.

For that reason, those striving to have a minimalist marriage would be wise to make sure they are **making their spouse feel appreciated.** It is the bare minimum requirement of a happy marriage.

You can do this in two ways: a) through words and b) through deeds.

We all love to hear "thank you." We all love to be thanked or praised in front of others, whether friends, family or our kids. So do that for your spouse. Make sure to acknowledge and praise them for the work they do or the person they are. Do it in front of others too, especially your children. Your spouse will love it.

After all, parenting can be a thankless job at times. Let your spouse know that you appreciate all they do and that you're trying to make your kids appreciate it, too.

Yet don't stop at speaking your appreciation. Show it, too. If you know your partner is overworked, offer to bring take-out home for dinner.

If your co-workers ask you to join them for a drink after work, call your partner first to make sure it's a good time. This isn't asking permission, it's being polite and appreciating the fact that your spouse may have something on the go.

Appreciation isn't just saying "thank you." It's showing your spouse that they are your priority, and that their happiness and well-being are always on your mind. It's showing your spouse that they truly matter.

## BRIGHT IDEA #17

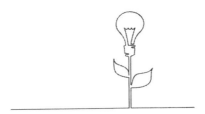

In my practice, I see a lot of infidelity and breaches of trust. I see a lot of people get swept up in the excitement or ego boost of an intimate friendship, emotional or physical affair, or even a strictly online affair.

While the reasons people stray from their marriage can be many and complex, there is one common and very simple reason: people cheat because of the way the other person makes them feel about themselves.

That's why it's so important to make your spouse feel good! **Minimalist marriages distill larger concepts down to their simplest form. So don't complicate matters. Just make your spouse feel good about themselves.**

There are many ways to do that, including making them feel respected and appreciated.

Another way is to **make your spouse feel desirable.** Sexy. Appealing. All spouses want to feel this way. And if you don't make your spouse feel like that, you are leaving them vulnerable to someone who will.

So flirt with your spouse. Flatter them. Steal a glance and offer them a loving yet mischievous smile. Send them a suggestive text. Keep that spark alive in your marriage.

That includes keeping your sex life alive. Emotional and sexual intimacy are two sides of the same coin. Both have value.

The sexual "spice it up" industry is teeming with tips to keep your sex life hot and heavy. That isn't necessarily a bad thing. If you've been together a long time, it can be a challenge to keep things fresh or come up with new ideas. Checking out a few new sex tips isn't any different than checking out a few new meal tips when you've been cooking the same dishes for years.

But if you're striving for a minimalist marriage, there really are only a few things you need to remember to keep your sex life healthy and happy:

1. Frequency. Many factors can impact sexual frequency, from exhaustion and lifestyle habits to natural aging and medical issues, and everything in between.

If you're not having sex as often as you used to or as often as you'd like, work with your spouse to pinpoint the reason and problem-solve.

Whether it's visiting your doctor, getting in better shape or simply going to bed earlier, you and your spouse should work together to ensure that sex doesn't fall off the radar in your marriage.

2. Variety. Variety is the spice of life. It's the spice of sex, too. Sexual familiarity and routine – where you can predict all of your partner's twists and turns – is a real passion-slayer.

Focus on bringing variety and unexpected pleasures to sex. Brushing up on your sexual technique, trying new positions, reading erotica or experimenting with erotic aides is a good start. Being intimate at different times and in different places can help, too.

3. Enthusiasm. Good sexual skill and technique is important; however, sexual enthusiasm is just as important. Nobody likes a lazy or apathetic partner who just "lies there" or who looks like they're bored by lovemaking.

We want to be with a partner who loses themselves in the pleasure and excitement of the experience. That kind of sexual enthusiasm is contagious and can bring a lot of energy to sex.

4. Respect. Sharing one's naked body in a sexually intimate way is a profoundly vulnerable experience. Spouses must take great care to respect each other's bodies, feelings and sensitivities during sex.

5. Mutual pleasure. Selfish lovers are no fun. Not only is sexual selfishness a turn-off, it is also an immature and narcissistic quality that can quickly chip away at a couple's intimacy.

When it comes to sex, both spouses should strive to put their partner's pleasure before their own. A spouse who feels like his or her pleasure is being prioritized is far more likely to prioritize his or her partner's pleasure.

# BRIGHT IDEA #18

Let me ask you this: have you ever made a mistake? Have you ever said something stupid or thoughtless? Have you ever knocked over a glass of water or made an innocent oversight?

Of course you have. We all have.

Now let me ask you this: have you ever had to apologize to someone who just wouldn't let it go? Who insisted on making a mountain of a molehill, as the expression goes? Who overreacted or was ultrasensitive or who seemed to reject your apology just for the sake of drama?

Of course you have. We all have.

Please, don't be that person!

**Couples in a minimalist marriage know one thing for certain: most things just aren't worth fighting about.**

If your spouse makes an innocent mistake or oversight, let it go. If they run over a skateboard while pulling into the garage, or knock over the milk carton, or burn dinner, or record the wrong television show, let it go.

Even better, laugh it off.

Having a minimalist marriage means minimizing needless conflict. So pick your battles. When you do, you'll discover that there's really not all that much worth fighting about.

## Bright Idea #19

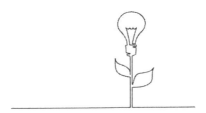

I've already talked about the importance of always speaking to your spouse in a respectful, loving tone of voice (see bright idea #6). It's true that our voice tone can influence the way our spouse hears what we're saying, regardless of the specific words we choose.

At the same time, there are certain words that we are wise to leave out of our married vocabulary altogether. To some extent, we all need to **choose our words** carefully.

Words that are spoken as insults or as character assassination should be heavily censored in a minimalist marriage. So too should words that are basically used for name-calling. And at the risk of coming across as a cheerless puritan, I would encourage you to avoid profanity, particularly if you're having an argument. Things can deteriorate fast enough without adding the harshness that swear words convey. It just doesn't help.

In addition to being more aware of your voice tone and word choice, I want you to catch yourself if you find that you're excessively repeating certain words or expressions when you speak to your partner, especially if you're having an argument or expressing a complaint.

Not only will your partner begin to tune you out, but you'll quickly feel exasperated and powerless. If you've said something two or three times to no effect, either rephrase what you've said or stop talking altogether and try a different approach.

## Bright Idea #20

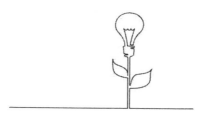

Our emotions can sometimes get the better of us. We might raise our voice a little too loudly, slam a cupboard or burst into tears. We might hang-up on our spouse or shut-down and give them the silent treatment. Nobody's perfect and we all have our bad days.

But in some cases, it goes beyond this. Some people make emotional outbursts – whether it's anger, tears or cold silence – a habit. These people are absolutely no fun to live with. And if you're one of them, you need to know that your spouse is falling out of love with you a little more each day.

There's just too much drama.

Yet take heart. Today is a new day and **your transition to a minimalist marriage involves ridding yourself of emotional outbursts that clutter your marriage with conflict** and resentment.

To that end, let's take a quick look at what happens before, during and after an outburst. The so-called anger escalation cycle (see the following image) is well-known; however, for our minimalist purposes, we can assume that most emotional outbursts follow this general pattern in a similar way…so whether you yell, cry or shut down, this cycle will likely resonate with you.

An emotional outburst can happen quickly or it can build up over minutes, days, even weeks. Regardless, you know it's happening and so does your spouse. You can feel it within you, and your spouse may feel like they have to walk on eggshells.

If it's your spouse that tends to have these outbursts, then it may be you who is choosing your words or doing what you can to prevent their behavior from escalating. You've seen it all play out before, and you're just not in the mood to deal with it.

Note: if you ever feel that your or your partner's emotions are too intense, or if you feel they are truly worrisome or threatening to you, them or anyone else, you need to reach out for the proper kind of help (i.e. a mental health expert, the police, a lawyer). Such situations are beyond the scope of this book. Here, we are talking about fairly common behavior that, although certainly unpleasant and unflattering, is not dangerous or abusive.

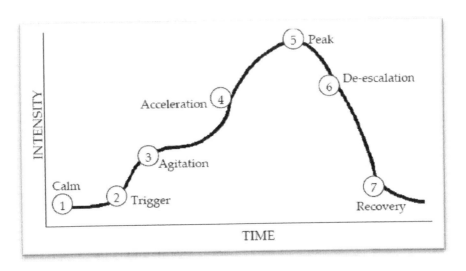

A person's emotional outburst usually starts with some kind of emotional trigger (2). This can be anything, whether it originates from within the marriage, outside the marriage or even inside the person's own mind. It can be an event, a memory, a feeling, an assumption, etc.

Common emotions that trigger an outburst and move a person from a state of calm (1) to a state of agitation (2) are things like feeling unheard, unappreciated, unimportant or disrespected.

Once a person is triggered, they become agitated. This may show in any number of ways or it may not really show at all. Regardless, their negative emotions and thoughts begin to escalate or accelerate (4).

During this period, a person's ability to cooperate, think rationally, collaborate or to see or respect someone else's position is reduced. They are just too emotional, too focused on their own thoughts, feelings, assumptions and so on.

The peak of the cycle (5) is just that – the peak of their outburst. This is when the person is at their worst. How they behave really depends on their personality, habits and what they know they can get away with. One person might yell or slam a door, another might cry, another might storm away, another might threaten divorce or give the cold shoulder.

Eventually, the runaway feelings, thoughts and behaviors that attend this peak begin to subside and the person becomes to come down from it all. The de-escalation period (6) is that coming down or cooling off period.

And then finally there is the recovery phase (7). I've had many clients describe this as the "I can't believe I acted like that" phase.

That's because when cooler heads prevail and we look back on our own behavior, we can be quite surprised – and not pleasantly so – at the rude way we spoke to or treated our partner, or the immature way we behaved. Frankly, it can be quite embarrassing. It can also lead to a lot of guilt as we realize that we had no business treating our spouse that way.

So that's a very general look at how an emotional outburst may proceed. It's good to know this, since knowledge is power. The sooner you can understand what is happening to you and/or your partner, the sooner you can start to gain better self-control over these kinds of outbursts. I've found that many people find looking at the cycle – seeing it play out in black and white – is helpful in itself.

Yet in addition to "showing" you what is happening, I'd also like to offer a few practical tips that may help you reduce the frequency and severity of emotional outbursts in your marriage:

1. *Talk it out when things are calm.* There is absolutely no point trying to talk about your marriage problems or trying to tell your partner how their outburst / behavior is inappropriate when they have passed that trigger point. Once a person is agitated, once they are moving up to that peak, they aren't in any state to have a reasonable conversation.

    Yet this is precisely when too many people do try to talk out their problems! They wait until things are heated, until they're in a middle of an argument, and then they say things like, "calm down!" or "we need to talk about this!" and so on. They may launch into criticisms or accusations, they may try to explain how they feel or why they're upset, they may start asking questions or challenging their partner.

    None of this will work. It will only make matters worse. Trying to resolve conflict when conflict is at its worst just doesn't make logical sense.

    Instead, I strongly recommend that you save these kinds of serious "talk it out" conversations for periods of calm and, even better, happiness. Sit outside in the sunshine, share a cool drink and have a heart-to-heart with your spouse about how these outbursts are chipping away at your marriage. Make sure the conversation stays loving, respectful and positive. The goal isn't to criticize or make someone feel bad. The goal is to make both of you feel good.

2. *Know your triggers.* A person's outburst usually starts with some sort of emotional trigger. As I said earlier, a trigger can be just about anything, real or imagined. Yet there are a number of particular emotions that are very common triggers.

These are feelings of being:

- unheard
- unappreciated
- unimportant
- disrespected
- unloved
- fearful
- powerless
- rejected

Think about these. Are there any that resonate with you? Once you know why you trigger, once you understand what feelings are fueling your outburst, you can brainstorm ways to manage those triggers and stay ahead of them.

What needs to happen in your marriage or in your own life, what needs to change, so that you can trigger less?

If you can keep the conversation positive and purposeful (remember that sunshine!) this can be a very useful thing for you and your spouse to work on together.

In the spirit of humility and love, identify your own and one another's triggers, and then come up with ways to avoid or reduce them. **A minimalist marriage should contain very few emotional triggers.**

3. *Remember the recovery phase.* You'll recall that some of my clients call the recovery phase the "I can't believe I acted like that" phase. The truth is, we can act in some very unflattering ways when we're agitated or at that peak. These are ways that, looking back, can make us feel embarrassed and guilty.

Well, if you're going to feel that way anyway (and you are!) why not use those bad feelings for good? Instead of trying to push the memory of the unflattering thing you said or did out of your mind, remember it. Use it as motivation to get a grip on your own behavior and to treat your spouse better.

If it's your partner who has outbursts and who is in the habit of apologizing to you in that recovery phase, don't say "oh, it's okay, I know you were upset." Be kind and respectful, but let them know that their outbursts are not okay. They need to know that and they need to do something about it.

## Bright Idea #21

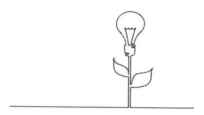

An argument is an ugly thing. I mean, just picture the look on someone's face when you're arguing with them: their lips are tight, their eyes are narrowed and their face is contorted.

Now imagine the face you're looking at is your own.

In fact, don't just imagine it. Get up, take this book into the bathroom, and **look at yourself in the mirror**. Really do it.

Think back to an argument or some unpleasant interaction that you've had with your spouse. If nothing comes to mind, make something up.

While looking in the mirror, I want you to pretend that your spouse is right in front of you and you're talking to them. Use the same expressions, the same words, the same voice tone you tend to use when you're at your most unpleasant.

How do you look? I'm willing to bet that you don't look your best. Well, guess what? That's what your spouse is seeing when you are at your worst.

It's been said that a picture says a thousand words and that's absolutely true. I could use a thousand words to describe what your partner is seeing when you are arguing or unkind, but it won't have the impact of you actually seeing what your partner is seeing.

This little exercise can also help reduce the emotional outbursts in your marriage (see bright idea #20) and help you get your extremes of emotion under control.

Why? Because once you see what your partner sees, you may want to start painting a different picture.

So let's do that now.

Close your eyes for a moment. When you open them, I want you to look in the mirror again. This time, smile. Let your eyes convey a sense of warmth and affection. Laugh. Pretend that you are saying something flattering or funny to your spouse.

How do you look? I'm willing to bet that you look great. And I'll bet your spouse would think so, too.

I used to keep a mirror in my office desk and every once in a while, if the case called for it, I'd pull it out and ask a client to do this exercise right in front of me.

"Look in the mirror," I'd say, "and then say what you said to your spouse, in the same way that you said it."

The result was always the same. The person would do it and then quickly put the mirror down, saying something like, "oh my god." Their regret was palpable. But so was their motivation to change for the better.

I've had countless clients tells me that this one simple exercise was more insightful to them than months of counseling, more useful than a dozen marriage books.

And for that reason, it's the perfect exercise for a minimalist marriage.

# Bright Idea #22

*Nosce te ipsum.* Know thyself. It's a Delphic maxim: the god Apollo commanded that humans do it.

Socrates said, "The unexamined life is not worth living."

People and powers greater than us have extolled the virtues of a thoughtful life. Of self-analysis.

It's a simple truth that **happy people make happy partners**.

So I have to ask: are you happy? If so, why? If no, why not?

When I was in law school, we once had a guest speaker who came to talk to us about happiness. He said that we should circle one date every month on our calendar, and that we should write on it: Am I happy?

At the time, I was a young law student. So, you know, fairly obnoxious. I thought I had all the answers and his advice seemed fluffy and pointless.

Now I see the wisdom in it. **The *minimalist* wisdom.**

Ask yourself: Am I happy? If the answer is yes, be grateful for the things and people that make you happy and treat them well. If the answer is no, it's time to do some soul-searching.

Most of us don't need a counselor or coach or guru to help us discover who we are or what makes us happy or unhappy. In my humble opinion at least, that's part of life and it's something that each of us has to take responsibility for.

If you aren't happy, there is no doubt that your unhappiness comes from somewhere and that it is affecting those around you. It's affecting your spouse and marriage, your kids and family life.

So do some soul-searching. Reach back into your past to see how it's affecting the choices you're making today and the person you are today.

Do some self-checking. What are your positive personality traits? What are your negative ones? How are those affecting the choices you make and the person you are? How are those affecting the other people in your life?

It doesn't have to be more complicated than this. You don't need to scale a mountaintop for enlightenment or rely on someone else to show you the way. You're capable. It's your life. Make it happy one and your marriage will be happier.

## BRIGHT IDEA #23

A minimalist marriage comes with a number of unexpected benefits. Not only will you cut down on the needlessly troublesome, time-consuming and costly parts of your life, you'll also find that you have more peace. More peace of mind. More peaceful interactions.

You can embrace this peaceful state even more by making a conscious effort to **lose the sense of urgency you feel when faced with a marriage issue**.

Remember: most marriage problems are not "emergencies." If you are angry or annoyed with your spouse, you don't have to "argue it out" or resolve it at that moment. It's okay to step back, to look at the big picture, to sleep on it and to think long-term.

Accept that you are going to have many bumps in the road in your relationship, especially if it's a long-term one. If you treat each one like the end of the journey, or if you rush to resolve it so you can "move on," you're going to run into trouble again and again.

So slow down. Embrace a more patient, peaceful vibe in your marriage. Resist the urge to react on impulse to every little thing. Instead, make it a habit to respond in a deliberate, respectful and thoughtful way. There's a saying in Latin: *Cogitationes posteriores sunt saniores.* It means "second thoughts are best."

This simple idea can prevent resentments and stressors from piling up in your marriage.

# Bright Idea #24

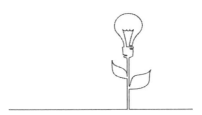

Not too long ago, my husband and I were having dinner at a lovely seaside restaurant. We were sitting outside on the patio under the sun, sipping our wine and watching the birds skim the water. Ah, sounds perfect, doesn't it? Sounds like the kind of afternoon that anyone would enjoy, right?

Wrong.

I couldn't help but notice the couple sitting a few tables away from us. They didn't speak a word to each other. They just sat there, avoiding eye contact, playing with their food and nursing their drinks until the bill came. And then they got up and left without a word to each other. They looked bored out of their minds.

I'll be honest. I felt a little bit of panic. Like most people who have been married a long time, I worry that some day we'll have nothing to talk about! That's especially so when some of the things that have dominated your marital conversations for so long – careers, kids – aren't as front and center as they used to be.

**As you're reducing the clutter in your marriage, I want you to increase something else – the "interesting" factor.** Make your minimalist marriage an interesting marriage.

Have shared interests. Something you can be curious about, talk about, look forward to. Maybe it's hiking or spelunking or bird-watching. Maybe it's astronomy or cooking or learning another language. It doesn't matter. Just keep your marriage interesting.

You should also have different interests. Maybe your spouse is into restoring old radios or riding a motorbike while you're into sci-fi movies or writing a book.

It doesn't matter whether your partner shares your interest to the point of wanting to jump in and join you. The truth is, people who have a passion for something are enjoyable company.

I used to go to school with a girl who was really into collecting snow globes – something I had zero interest in. Nonetheless, whenever she talked about snow globes or showed you a snow globe, she could hardly contain her excitement.

She'd go on about the different types of manufacturing and the various kinds of glitter, how to replace the water if it started to leak or get murky, and so on.

And to this day, decades later, whenever I see a snow globe I have to stop and pick it up. Is it plastic or glass? Does it have a music box? What is the material used to make the landscape? What kind of glitter is used? Is it just a mass-produced snow globe from China or is it a finely crafted snow globe from Austria?

I can't say that snow globes are a passion of mine. I can say, however, that my friend's passion for snow globes was contagious. It drew you in. It made you interested, by association, in what she was interested in. But more than that, it made you interested in her as a person. Her passion drew you in. She had a strong personality and that was very appealing.

Finally, be sure to show interest in your spouse's life. We all love to feel that someone finds us interesting, unique or special. I've heard many people tell me that they were drawn to a woman or man outside the marriage because of the way this other person make them feel about themselves. The other woman or the other man showed interest in them and in their life. We can lose that over the years in marriage, but I urge you to rediscover it.

A minimalist marriage keeps the essentials. Having an interesting marriage, being interested in each other, are essentials.

## BRIGHT IDEA #25

There are many things that can clutter a marriage and make it difficult to move past problems or enjoy a happy, healthy marriage that works for both spouses. Fear is one of the biggest things.

For example, I see a lot of infidelity in my practice and I often find that fear is the one thing preventing a marriage from recovering in a truly mature and authentic way.

Take the case of a middle-aged woman who discovers that her husband is having an affair with another woman. She insists that he end it immediately or she'll move out, but he refuses.

Instead of following through with the consequence and moving out, she hesitates. She's fearful. She's afraid that if she leaves the family home, her husband won't care and will only grow closer to his affair partner.

She's afraid that if she leaves, he will choose his affair partner over her. She's afraid of losing him, losing her lifestyle and marital identity, of being a divorced woman at her age. Maybe she'll never meet another man. Maybe she will be miserable while he will be happier than ever.

All of these are such scary scenarios that she does nothing. She lives in a chronic state of anxiety and heartache while her husband carries on an emotional and sexual affair with another woman. After all, why would he end it? He doesn't have to.

This is just one example of many.

It is just as often a husband who hesitates to reasonably and respectfully assert himself in his marriage for fear that his wife will leave him.

He may be afraid to lose her to another man, to lose their years of marriage, to lose access to his kids or the assets he's worked so hard for.

Obviously, I'm mentioning this here in the most superficial way possible. The reasons for infidelity and the impact it has on spouses and marriage is well beyond the scope of this book.

My point here is simply to illustrate how fear can clutter an issue and how it can lead to ongoing drama in a marriage. A spouse who is too afraid to make a change will never see a change.

This spouse doesn't have the clarity, the strength or the self-determination to act in their own best interests or to prompt the kind of change that is necessary for their marriage to be a truly happy, loving and respectful one.

Facing one's fears is one of those things that we all have to do both in life and in marriage. Marriage makes us vulnerable. When you love someone, you are of course afraid to lose them.

Yet to keep our marriage strong and stable, to limit the drama, we need to face that fear.

As with other life and marital issues you'll find in this book, much has been written on facing one's fears. From self-help books to hypnosis, it's easy to get overwhelmed with clutter and overly complicated solutions that only seem to prolong the situation.

**In the interests of having a minimalist approach to this, I'd like to offer a simple ten-step process that can help you face (and face down!) your fears of relationship failure.** And the funny part is, the more you can do that, the more successful your marriage can be.

10 Steps to Face Your Fears of Relationship Failure:

1. Identify and itemize your fears.

2. Realize that you have already successfully lived through fear in your life, and you're still successfully living through fear – all kinds of fear, not just the fear of relationship failure. Remind yourself of a fear that you have overcome, or at least learned to successfully live with.

3. Embrace the exhilaration of conquering a fear – any fear! Is there another fear, something other than your fear of relationship failure, that you can conquer? It can help to remind you of how good it feels to do this.

4. Be aware of your own body and how it responds to fear. This kind of awareness can help you feel less afraid and more in control.

5. Challenge your assumptions that your "worst-case scenario" will come true. What (fear-based) assumptions are you making?

6. Educate yourself. It may help to do some fact-gathering so that you can challenge your assumptions or worst-case scenarios. What facts might you need to gather?

7. Give yourself an attitude-adjustment. There are situations where having a "bring it on" attitude, or even an empowering "chip on your shoulder" can help a person see a situation differently and protect themselves from harm. In what ways might you be in need of an attitude adjustment? How can you do this in a practical, positive way?

8. When you begin to become less fearful and more empowered, the way you see yourself, your spouse and the situation may change. You may change. And it is likely your spouse will notice the change. How might this reverberate in the marriage? How might your spouse react to this? Does your spouse want you to change like this? Why or why not?

9. Always use your newfound "courage" (and clarity) for good, not evil! Use it to have more self-determination and a better marriage, not to prove how tough you are to your spouse. Think about it – how can you use your newfound courage for good?

10. Give your fear a purpose. Fear isn't always bad. It can have a purpose. It can motivate us to take better care of ourselves and to make changes – in our marriage and in our life in a larger sense – that can make us happier. Is there anything "positive" that fear has ever motivated you to do?

This kind of exercise may not apply to anything that is happening in your marriage right now. In fact, I hope it doesn't!

But conflict is unavoidable in marriage and sometimes serious conflict, perhaps a spouse's overly intimate opposite-sex friendship or something similar, can trigger a fear reaction that keeps us mired in conflict and unhappiness, and that burdens our marriage with clutter.

If that happens to you, don't panic. Don't let your fear take over or cloud your clear-thinking or choices. People in minimalist marriages like to be in control over their own lives. Use that spirit of empowerment to make your marriage a truly fearless one.

## BRIGHT IDEA #26

While a minimalist marriage usually strives to have less of something, there are some things you certainly want to have more of. More peace of mind, more money in the bank, more time to relax and spend with friends and family, more love and more commitment from your spouse.

Another thing that you should try to have more of – particularly during times of marital conflict – is perspective. **The more perspective you have, the less mind-clutter you will have.**

Mind-clutter is all those fears (see bright idea #25), doubts, speculations and assumptions (see bright idea #28) that make us lose our perspective and obsess about our marriage problems to the point that we can't even see them clearly or think clearly about them.

It's when our mind races with worst-case scenarios and "what if's," when it replays a situation or interaction over and over again, so that we can't see things as they really are. We can't problem-solve since the problem seems too diffuse, too complex.

And it's especially when we start to think that this one problem – whether a marriage problem or something else – is the only thing that matters in our life. This one problem gets so big, so complicated, that there just isn't room in our thoughts for anything else. Our mind is too cluttered.

If this resonates with you, you might need a good dose of perspective. It's an essential part of a minimalist marriage.

One of my favorite movies is a little cult film *called Joe versus the Volcano*. To make a long story short, Joe finds himself lost at sea, floating for days on end on top of some luggage he's managed to fasten together. He's exposed to the raging heat of day and his skin is blistered from the sun. He's out of drinking water. He's certain that he's going to die.

And then one black night, the moon rises above him – it's massive and takes up 2/3 of the movie screen. Despite knowing that death is around the corner, he stumbles to his feet and looks up at it, filled with a sudden fascination and gratitude for his own life.

He says, "Thank you for my life – I forgot how big!"

It's a scene I'll sometimes share with clients, especially ones that I have a good rapport with and who seem to need a dose of perspective.

During times of conflict, always remember that your life is bigger than this. Do not let this one event define your life. Do not let it compromise your career or your relationship with your kids. I don't say this lightly, but you need to have some perspective. If you don't, your marriage problem can consume you and add even more drama to your life.

It's also important to have perspective in terms of the relationship between you and your spouse. Your marriage is bigger than any one marriage conflict or event. The story of you and spouse is a long one, with many chapters, not just one.

How you find perspective is really up to you. It might depend on your beliefs, personality or preferences. I find that humor gives me a lot of perspective. You might find that your faith, charity work, physical exercise or meditation does the trick.

It doesn't matter how you do it. Just remember that a successful minimalist marriage keeps everything in perspective.

## BRIGHT IDEA #27

There is one characteristic of a successful minimalist marriage that is so boring, so excruciatingly prosaic, that I almost don't want to mention it lest you think I am of the hopelessly unimaginative variety.

But I have to.

And that characteristic is…wait for it…*reliability*.

I know, big yawn.

Yet when we imagine a marriage without this, we realize what a relationship pillar it really is. Without it, it all comes crashing down. Unreliable partners are the worst of all partners. The amount of chaos, clutter and conflict they can bring to a marriage is nothing short of staggering.

In the best of cases, their thoughtlessness creates an unending series of inconveniences that can make their spouse feel annoyed and disrespected.

They might forget to pick up something important they were asked to pick up. They might not show up for a social or family event, or they might wander in an hour late. They might say something rude or embarrassing at your Christmas work party.

In the worst of cases, their unreliability dips into untrustworthiness. They are liars. They are secret, selfish spenders. They are cheaters. They are checked-out parents and immature spouses.

Unreliable partners bring an incredible amount of stress and uncertainty to a marriage. I've had clients say, "What happens if I get sick? There's no way she can take care of everything" or "I live in fear that he'll forget to pick the kids up from daycare" or "I don't trust her when she's gone on a work trip."

It's impossible to relax or feel reassured when you can't rely on your spouse. It's impossible to feel like you have a real relationship at all.

You may have seen this in action with a couple you know. Maybe you have a friend or co-worker whose husband or wife is always letting them down, always forgetting something, always causing some crisis or another. There's just always some drama going on, isn't there?

Of all the bright ideas in this book, I think that reliability is the brightest. It's the foundation of a minimalist marriage because everything else is built on top of it. **If you're going to start practicing the various monetary, marital and lifestyle elements that are necessary to have a minimalist marriage, you must be able to rely on each other.**

Be a reliable spouse. If you can already rely on your partner, be sure to thank them for that and show your appreciation. It may sound boring, but it's the best indicator of a fabulous marriage.

If your spouse isn't the most reliable person, don't just criticize or complain. Let them know how you feel and then offer to brainstorm ways you can strengthen that foundation of your marriage. Some people are just forgetful and do need some pointers. That's especially true in new marriages where we're still making that transition from singlehood to couplehood (or parenthood).

When you see your partner making an effort, thank them and show your appreciation. Let them know how much it means. That can motivate a spouse to do more of the same. "Hey, that made her happy…I'll remember that." If they can rely on your positive reinforcement, perhaps they will become more reliable themselves.

# BRIGHT IDEA #28

Years ago, I was consulting with a separated couple in my office. They were a young urban couple in their early twenties and their new marriage – they'd only been married a year – was going through some growing pains.

Apparently, they had been arguing one night when the wife said to the husband, "I'm so frustrated. Maybe I should just go stay at my mom's tonight."

The husband replied by saying, "Okay. Would you like me to call you a taxi?"

At that, the wife grabbed her things, stormed out of the house and for a week straight refused to take her husband's phone calls. He had finally persuaded her to meet him at my office.

It didn't take long for the clouds to part and for this couple to understand what went wrong that night. In a word: assumption.

When the wife had said, "I'm so frustrated. Maybe I should just go stay at my mom's tonight," she had assumed her husband would respond with something like, "I don't want you to go. Let's work this out." She had wanted to hear that from him. She was looking for some reassurance.

Yet when the husband heard her say this, he assumed that she meant what she said. He assumed that she really needed some space. And so in an effort to support her, he offered to call her a taxi; however, he didn't really want her to go.

Of course, his wife didn't know that. She made the assumption that he wanted her to go. That he didn't care enough to ask her to stay. So instead of getting the reassurance that she was seeking and hoping for, she felt even more insecure.

Now, never mind the obvious communication mistakes here. Those are evident and this particular couple did a wonderful job of working on those.

My point in sharing this story is to showcase just how off-base and destructive assumptions can be. They can bring more unnecessary drama and confusion to a situation that almost anything else. In this case, they almost drove a permanent wedge between two people who were actually very much in love with each other.

**Couples in a minimalist marriage should keep their assumptions to a bare minimum.** When you feel that little twinge of confusion, don't jump to an assumption. When your spouse says or does something that doesn't quite add up, clarify. Talk about it.

When you don't have all the information about something – say, why your partner isn't answering a text at work – don't fill in the blanks with some worst-case scenario, like they're sharing a private lunch with a hot new co-worker.

We all make assumptions. Yet isn't it strange that when it comes to our spouse, we too often jump to a negative assumption before a positive one?

If we walk into the room and our spouse quickly shuts down the computer, we might assume they were looking at something shady or talking to someone they shouldn't be. We may be less likely to assume they were planning a surprise romantic getaway.

A word to the wise is sufficient here. Minimizing assumptions is one of the most powerful and practical ways to reduce the number of misunderstandings in your marriage, and to avoid the kind of needless drama that this young couple experienced.

## Bright Idea #29

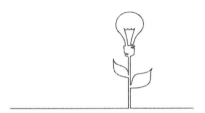

I once had a very animated colleague who gave me a piece of marriage advice that I've never forgotten (and that I still practice). She said, "Don't let your husband see you naked too often. He won't think it's special anymore."

It sounded funny coming from her, but even back then, when I was newlywed myself, I could see the flash of wisdom in it.

Personally, I do think it's important to keep some "mystery" going in a marriage. I know people have different habits and comfort levels, but – forgive me – it just isn't sexy to leave the bathroom door open when you're on the toilet.

Professionally, I have had clients complain that their partner has gotten just a little too…ahem…comfortable with the noises that come from their own body.

Of course, there are times we can't help it. We get sick or we get food poisoning. Things can get nasty enough that the neighbors can hear what's happening. We don't always look or smell good. The human body isn't always on its best behavior and part of being married is being mature enough to accept each other for better or for worse, and to stand by each other through all of it.

But you get where I'm going with this. **A minimalist marriage should strive to keep some mystery alive.**

# BRIGHT IDEA #30

Minimalist marriages seek to cut down on things that a couple just doesn't need. Debt and arguments are two such things and this bright idea can help you reduce both at the same time.

**Have a purchase limit.**

More specifically, have two types of purchase limits.

The first type is your "one spouse" purchase limit. This is the maximum amount of money that a spouse can spend without having to check with the other spouse.

The amount of this will depend entirely on your preferences as a couple and your financial situation. For some couples who are struggling to reduce debt, this purchase limit may be as low as $50.00. Any amount greater than that, and the purchasing partner has to call their spouse to get the okay.

There may be exceptions to this purchase limit, such as groceries or other budgeted for items (see bright idea #12) and emergency situations.

The second type is your "couple" purchase limit. This is the maximum amount of money that you can spend as a couple without first "sleeping on it."

For example, a couple who is struggling to get impulse purchases under control may decide to have a couple purchase limit of $200.00. Any amount greater than that, and they must first go home and sleep on it to avoid buying things they don't need.

If they wake up the next morning and decide the purchase is still a wise or necessary one, then great. Back to the store (or online store) they go.

As long as both spouses agree to the purchase limit amounts, and as long as the amounts are realistic, this simple habit can seriously cut down on frivolous spending, debt and the amount of clutter in your home.

As importantly, it can cut down on the number of money-related arguments that you and your spouse have.

## BRIGHT IDEA #31

*Tempus fugit.* It's Latin for "time flies."

The philosopher William Penn famously said, "Time is what we want most, but what we use worst."

And Shakespeare: "I wasted time, now doth time waste me."

Indeed, of all the things we waste in life and in marriage – things, money, opportunity – the worst thing of all to waste is time.

I think that's what draws most couples to a minimalist marriage in the first place: the desire to have more time, more quality time, more time to enjoy each other and to explore the world the way we want to explore it.

**Time on our own terms.**

When I see a couple making unnecessary large purchases (see bright idea #1) or otherwise spending their money needlessly, I want to say to them, "Wait! Do you really want to spend another five or ten or twenty years of your life working to pay for *that*? Isn't there something else you'd rather do with your time?"

When I see parents making unnecessary purchases, I think, "Now you have to spend your time paying for *that* instead of playing with your kids."

That's just the way it is. You can't be two places at once. You can't be at the office working to pay for your stuff and walking on the beach with your kids or spouse or dog at the same time.

Of course, there are things we need to buy and things we simply want to buy. They're worth it to us. Some possessions, providing you can afford them and they fit into your lifestyle or interests, have great value and can make you very happy.

**The point of minimalism is to be selective**. To avoid excessive, burdensome things that bring no physical, mental or emotional value to your life, but that instead add clutter and conflict to your life. The kind of clutter and conflict that ends up costing you something – money, time, stress, regret, even illness – instead of truly paying off in some way.

So the next time you are going to buy something, just pause for a moment and ask yourself: Is this item worth my time? Does it add physical, mental or emotional value to my life or marriage in some way? If no, don't buy it. If yes, pull out your wallet.

All right. I want to shift gears now and talk about time in a different way – in terms of timing. Good timing and bad timing. Because knowing the difference, being able to quickly recognize the difference, is a vital skill in a minimalist marriage.

Good timing is especially important when it comes to communication, since it can prevent all kinds of relationship drama.

Take the case of a husband who one night stumbles upon an unusual text message on his wife's phone from someone named "Thomas." It says: *Looking forward to seeing you again on Thursday!* He says nothing but it sticks in his mind.

They go to bed, but he stays up thinking about it, making all kinds of assumptions. And then, at the peak of his worry and dire speculations – which happens to occur at three o'clock in the morning – he wakes up his wife and says, "Who is this from?"

Instantly, she's mad. First, the text was a reminder for an appointment at the dentist – Dr. Thomas's office. Second, it's three o'clock in the morning and she was just woken from a dead sleep. It's almost inevitable that an argument is going to happen. And all because of bad timing.

It may be that it was only the late hour that made this normally level-headed husband focus on this text. If he had seen it in the morning, he might have dismissed it altogether or simply assumed his wife had some kind of appointment and gone about his day without giving it a second thought.

Yet even if he had a legitimate concern about the text or the marriage, his poor timing made it very unlikely that his wife would be willing to talk it out with a cooperative spirit.

Too many couples are governed entirely by their emotions. If something is making them upset, they feel compelled to talk about at that moment (see bright idea #23) regardless of whether the timing is right or not.

You've seen those couples who argue in public, right? They'll have an argument in the parking lot of a restaurant, in the auditorium of their child's school, even on the beach while on vacation. The combination of poor self-control and bad timing is making things a lot messier than they have to be.

Working with couples, I've found a common complaint is that one spouse will call their partner at their place of work and they'll have an argument over the phone. I've even had cases where an angry spouse showed up at their partner's workplace to argue or make some kind of accusation that "just couldn't wait."

Well, most things can wait.

So have good timing. Don't wake your partner up in the middle of the night to talk, don't call them at work or show up at their office, don't argue in public.

Choose the right time, the right mood and the right attitude.

Bad timing can inflame a marriage problem and lead to drama. It can also create a bunch of pointless offshoot problems that cause even more conflict and clutter.

Good timing can eliminate a marriage problem and lead to happiness. Always practice good timing in your minimalist marriage.

# BRIGHT IDEA #32

Individuals or couples who want to improve their marriage or resolve a specific marriage problem often consult multiple resources to do that: counseling, coaching, books, marriage systems, spiritual advisors and so on.

What they will often find is that they're assigned some kind of "homework" or exercise to complete as a couple. And guess what? Nobody does it. Or if they do, it's one partner doing it while the other procrastinates and refuses…and then they argue about that!

Plus, I've had some clients say that the marriage counseling exercises they were assigned actually made things worse. I remember one couple came in after being told to have an "honesty hour." During this hour, they were to tell their partner every little thing they didn't like about them or wanted them to change (see bright idea #7).

Of course, they were advised to do this "without judgment, without getting angry or hurt." But of course they judged, got angry and hurt. Brutal, unfiltered honesty isn't always the best idea, especially in a marriage that's already filled with hard feelings.

I rarely assign any kind of couples homework or exercises when I see office clients. What I try to do instead is to make each partner take a critical look at their own behavior and try to figure out the situation on their own – after all, they know their spouse and marriage best. They know themselves best, too.

Why do I do this? Not because I'm trying to pass the buck. I do it because it's a low-conflict, lasting way to resolve problems.

Let me explain: when couples are in conflict, they are usually competing to be heard. To complain. To tell the other person how they are hurt or angry or whatever. As a result, a marriage practitioner can often find themselves in the role of a referee as two self-focused people go at it. That wastes everyone's time.

Here are the only two things that *really* need to happen. First, each spouse needs to better understand what their partner is going through. Second, each spouse needs to be aware of how they are interacting with their spouse and contributing to the problem.

If both spouses are striving to do these two very basic things, reconciliation is faster, comprehensive, collaborative and lasting. There is absolutely no reason for marriage exercises to be complex or cutesy. That only adds clutter to an already complicated situation.

**I recommend that couples in a minimalist marriage try to limit their "marriage exercises" to what follows.** These short questions put the responsibility on you, as a spouse, to do the work it takes to understand and empathize with your partner. They put the responsibility on you, as a spouse, to assess your own behavior in the marriage.

Don't expect a third-person to solve your marriage problems for you. Nobody has all the answers and nobody knows you, your spouse or your marriage the way you do. Marriage is about working as a two-person team, so the more you can do that, the better.

A bonus of this minimalist approach to marriage is that spouses can see each other actually putting in the effort. They can see that their spouse cares enough about the marriage to be self-critical instead of just critical.

Spouses can see each other taking the time to better understand one another. That feels good! It's wonderful to know that our spouse wants to understand us better and is willing to do the work. That in itself can make a marriage stronger and happier.

To have a decent understanding of your partner, particularly in times of conflict, ask yourself these questions:

What might my spouse be:

Feeling      _____

Expecting      _____

Assuming      _____

Afraid of      _____

Needing      _____

Hoping for      _____

Thinking      _____

To have a decent understanding of how you relate to your partner, ask yourself these questions:

How have I been showing my spouse:

Love      _____

Friendship      _____

Appreciation      _____

Desire      _____

Support      _____

Devotion      _____

If you are currently in conflict (or the next time you are!) ask yourself these two simple questions:

How did I contribute to this conflict?

_____

_____

If I had a do-over, what would I do differently?

_____

_____

When it comes to working through a marriage problem, we need to keep things simple. Clear. Sincere. We do not want to complicate or cloud the issue. We do not want to get into a Him vs. Her match that relies on a referee to keep things moving.

In a minimalist marriage, both spouses will approach problems by first working through these questions, on their own. These are excellent and relevant starting points.

Then, when it's time to come together and talk, they will have already done a lot of the work it takes to solve the problem, get back on track and demonstrate their commitment to the marriage.

## BRIGHT IDEA #33

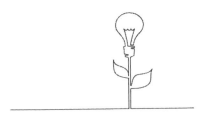

As I said in the welcome to this book, a minimalist marriage has a lot to offer, but it does ask one thing of you – change. And change is hard. Some people resist it. If you're here, however, it's more likely that you want change. You're up for it!

Yet you have a problem. Change requires, well, change. To have a successful minimalist marriage, you may need to change certain aspects of your lifestyle and spending habits (see bright ideas #1 and #12).

This will affect you, your spouse and your kids if you have any. It may affect the way you socialize with friends or extended family.

You may need to make changes to your banking or financial framework, to the way you get around, to where you live, to what you eat, to how you shop or have fun.

There may be a few or many changes, minor or major changes. They're all for the better, but that doesn't mean it won't take a bit of practical planning to get there. And that's where some couples drop the ball. They're motivated, intelligent and committed to a minimalist marriage; however, they aren't great at preparation or true follow-through.

Getting started is definitely the hardest part. Where to start? When it comes to getting organized and removing the barriers that are standing in the way of positive change, simplicity is essential.

That's why I want to present you with a very simple and straightforward flowchart to follow. As with so many things, it just doesn't have to be more complicated than this. Change may be hard, but at least this approach to change is easy:

## An 8-Step Process for Change

Step 1: Pinpoint the specific thing(s) you want to change
(i.e. reduce debt, get rid of junk and clutter around the house, have less food wastage)

Step 2: Gather necessary or relevant information
(i.e. How much debt are we in exactly? What are our various terms and interest rates? What items have we not used in over a year? What meals do we like best? What foods normally spoil in our fridge?)

Step 3: Brainstorm potential courses of action based the facts you have gathered
(i.e. downsize home, make a budget, sell or donate household items, reduce variety of grocery items purchased)

Step 4: Ask how each course of action will impact each spouse and family member
(i.e. selling the home may increase husband's work commute, reducing household items may be emotional or worrisome for kids, a smaller variety of grocery items make meal prep harder for wife)
This step – asking how each spouse or family member will be affected by change – is an all-important one. Remember that the goal is to reduce clutter and conflict. If change doesn't work for a spouse or child, it will only lead to more conflict. Propose changes and courses of action that everyone in the home is on board with.

Step 5:  Choose the best course of action
(i.e. reducing household items)

Step 6:  Delegate duties and responsibilities
(i.e. husband will focus on items in garage, wife will investigate charities that accept donations, kids will put stickers on household items / toys they want to donate or keep)

Step 7:  Support each other and celebrate progress.  Be sure to approach change and a more minimalist lifestyle with the right attitude.  If you find yourself saying, "You need to get rid of that!" to a spouse or child, bite your tongue.  Do your part.  You can encourage others to do theirs, but don't bully or pressure them.

Minimalism is a mindset as much as anything else.  Lead by example and show your spouse and your kids how empowering it is to live simply and to reduce the physical, emotional and mental clutter in your lives.

When you have success, celebrate it.  Talk about how good it feels to get rid of this or not worry so much about that.  Talk about how much more time or peace of mind you have.  Talk about the argument you didn't have because you've eliminated its source.  A minimalist marriage is a good thing.  Remind yourselves of that!

Step 8:  Have check-points.  Because it's all too easy to slip back into bad or at least more familiar habits, it's always a smart idea to have check-points to monitor your progress and re-inspire yourselves to stick to a minimalist marriage.

Circle the first and last dates of each month.  On the first day, recommit as partners (or as a family) to making this month count.  On the last day, look back on your progress.  Identify what you did right and what you did wrong.  Do this every month.

# BRIGHT IDEA #34

Minimalism is a way of life and a state of mind. Some people feel that minimalism has a spiritual element to it as well, since it symbolizes the way they want to interpret and experience life itself: on their own terms.

With simplicity and truth.

Without clutter and conflict.

If you're going to make a minimalist marriage work, I think it can be very useful to look for this kind of deeper meaning. Although I've spoken with many minimalists, I don't think I've ever spoken to one who said "Oh, I'm just doing this to save money" or "I just want to get rid of stuff."

There's always more to it. A philosophy.

What's your "more to it" reason?

That's not a rhetorical question. I really want you to think about it and answer it. Answer it as an individual and then answer it together, as a couple.

Get a little philosophical. **The more meaning you can find in what you're doing, the more successfully you will do it.**

## Bright Idea #35

In my capacity as a couples mediator and marriage conflict specialist, I've seen couples try countless ways to reduce the drama and increase the happiness in their marriage: books, marriage systems, hypnosis, spells, prayer, counseling, coaching, marriage exercises and couples retreats...hey, whatever works!

Unfortunately, many couples find that none of these things work. Maybe they were too theoretical. Maybe they were too complicated. Maybe they were too patronizing or fluffy.

Or maybe – and I think this is often the case – they enabled people to focus more on what their spouse is or isn't doing instead of what they themselves are doing or not doing.

**After all, the only person you can truly control is yourself. That realization is itself grounded in minimalism.**

Which brings me to a simple strategy that I often recommend to clients. Imagine yourself stepping into a time machine. I don't know what that would look like, so let's imagine this time machine looks like one of those big red phone boxes you see in London. You step in, close the door, spin around three times and then open the door....to another time and place.

This is the time and place where you and your spouse first met. So picture that – go there in your mind. Go back to the age you were, the city you lived in, where you worked or went to school.

Do your best to immerse yourself in the feeling and memory of that time. It was probably a simpler time, wasn't it? You and your husband or wife were still new to each other.

You were still in the infatuation stage of your relationship. You felt desire for each other and you looked past each other's flaws (if you saw them at all).

**I want you to remember and re-experience the feeling of what it was like to fall in love with your partner.** Because when it comes to falling in love, we all do it in our own way.

Now I want you to recall the way you used to talk to your spouse – your then boyfriend or girlfriend. How did you treat them? How much effort did you put into making them happy or making a good impression on them? What kind of voice tone did you use? What kind of words? How did you dress or present yourself?

Now step back into the time machine and return to today. What is different?

Is it possible that you've lost some of the softness or patience in your voice tone? Is it possible that you don't make as much effort these days to impress your spouse, to make them happy or to downplay conflict?

For many if not most couples, those early days of a relationship were simpler days. Sure, we had stressors and worries, but maybe not to the same degree.

Maybe things like kids, bills, the mortgage, career issues and the daily demands of domestic life have added clutter and conflict over the years. Maybe all that stuff has piled up so much that we have forgotten how we used to be.

If so, do a little time travel. Reach back to when times were simpler, to when you were a new couple, and bring the best of that time into your present life. That includes your own behavior.

To add even more impact to this experience, you can use the street view feature of Google maps to re-visit the places you and your partner used to go when times were simpler.

Take a visual stroll down memory lane. Visit the restaurant where you had your first date or the park where you used to walk well after dark, just enjoying each other's company under the stars. Let the romance of that time, including your own romantic behavior, come back to you.

Of all the marriage-strengthening exercises I've seen over the years, I really do believe this simple concept yields the best results, especially if both spouses are participating. It's a bright idea that a minimalist couple should keep in mind through each and every time period of their marriage.

## BRIGHT IDEA #36

You've heard the expression the couple that plays together stays together. No truer words were ever spoken.

Here's the thing, though. I think that a lot of couples don't "play" as hard as they could. Many couples do activities together – hiking, cooking, traveling, whatever. They have shared interests and they enjoy spending time together. That's great.

But it isn't really playing, is it? It isn't that "kid" type of play where you're giddy, where you're almost doubled over with laughter and the silliness of it all.

**I think it's important for couples to really *play* together.** To ride a roller coaster. The experience you have on a roller coaster – shrieking, feeling that rush of adrenaline and excitement – is very different than the pleasure you get from hiking or together.

Not too long ago, I was in a bit of a grumpy mood. We were out and about when Don took a detour.

I said, "Oh come on, let's just go home."

"Nope," he said. "We're doing this."

And so we went into (or rather, he dragged me into) a VR arcade. A virtual reality gaming center.

It was the last thing in the world I wanted to do. I was sour from the start. I didn't want to put the headset on. I didn't want to choose a game. But I did and, a moment later, I was immersed in another world, a world where zombies were attacking me.

It was terrifying, to be honest. When they say virtual "reality," they mean it. It looks real. It sounds real.

I screamed. I dropped to my knees. I got back up and started shooting zombies. I started *playing*. Even through my own cries and the snarls of the zombies I could hear Don laughing at me and I had to laugh, too. We were having fun. Kid fun.

While my husband and I have been moving more and more toward a minimalist marriage, we have actually added something to our home. A virtual reality gaming system.

This is a great example of a somewhat costly purchase that nonetheless suits a minimalist marriage just fine.

Remember, couples in a minimalist marriage are selective with their purchases (see bright idea #31). They spend their money on items that add physical, mental or emotional value to their marriage. For us, this purchase did. Even months later, we still regularly "play" with it and it's just as fun every time.

You and your spouse will have to find your own way to have fun. To play together. I simply remind you to strive for the kind of simple, pure fun that you used to have when you were kids. There is something fundamentally minimalist, and magical, about that.

## Bright Idea #37

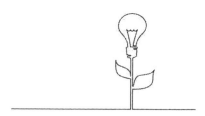

I make no secret of the fact that I'm not a fan of social media and particularly of the needless destruction it can cause in a marriage (see bright idea #5).

I also recommend very thoughtful and minimal use of personal technology, including phones and texting (see bright idea #10).

These things aren't just distracting. They also leave the door to your marriage wide open to the big bad world and the shady folks that populate it.

Still, I know these things aren't going anywhere and I know they are going to continue to cause relationship problems. That being the case, there is one very important thing you can do to make sure that technology doesn't lead to trust issues in your marriage.

**Share your passwords for all your devices and online accounts.**

No, it isn't a guarantee of trustworthiness. If a person is going to cheat they're going to cheat. But it is a trustworthy gesture and one that sends the message that neither of you have any secrets.

This should be a bare minimum rule in every relationship, whether it's a minimalist marriage or not.

## Bright Idea #38

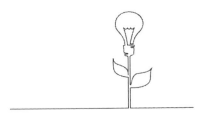

Have you and your spouse ever had an argument over text messages? If so, you know quickly things can get out of hand.

One of the many problems with text messages is that all the natural elements of a face to face conversation – voice tone, facial expression, body language, real-time back and forth – are missing. There are no tonal or visual clues to help us interpret what is being said or take it in the spirit in which it was intended.

It's too easy to assume that a joke was a jab or a question was a statement. It's too easy to assume that someone is being rude with a one-word response or that they're angry or punishing us when they don't reply right away.

It's too easy to let our emotions and assumptions get carried away. And when they do, there is no opportunity to have our spouse look into our eyes, hold our hand, and say, "that's not what I meant."

Things are a little better when it comes to telephone conversations; however, these are still rife with assumption and the potential for misunderstanding.

If we can't read someone's face, we aren't getting the whole story. That's why I believe couples in a minimalist marriage should agree that they will **only argue in person.**

Agreeing to argue only when you're face to face, when you can respond in real-time to what's really being said, can cut down on misunderstandings and runaway text fights.

Of course, this is easier said than done – but you need to do it anyway! Remind yourselves that not all marriage issues are emergencies (see bright idea #23) and try to have a big picture, long-term vision of your marriage.

If you can do that, you won't feel as compelled to talk it out when the timing is all wrong (see bright idea #31) and the circumstances are guaranteed to add unnecessary drama and conflict to your marriage.

## BRIGHT IDEA #39

When I was a kid, I remember thinking that my grandfather had way too much time on his hands. I recall sitting at the kitchen table eating a bowl of raspberries from my grandma's garden and watching him reach over the low white fence into the next yard to retrieve a toaster that his neighbor had thrown away.

He then spent half the day fixing the toaster and gave it to my grandma who polished it up and put it on the counter. It sat there for probably the next fifteen years. Making perfect toast every time.

My grandparents were definitely old school. They lived in one house for the fifty-plus years of their marriage. It was one of those tiny war-time homes.

From the earliest times I can remember until they passed (three months apart from one another), they used the same glasses, same plates, same cutlery, same pots and pans. I remember they bought a new couch – a chesterfield – but didn't throw out the old one. It went to the cabin.

My grandparents were of that generation that had actually gone hungry during the Great Depression. I remember my grandma telling me how my grandpa had jumped on a train to travel cross-country looking for work.

He left with one loaf of bread that was to last him a week. By the end of the week, it was so hard that it made his gums bleed.

It sounds like that Monty Python skit where the old guys one-up each other about how bad their childhoods were, about how poor they were and how rough they had it. One says he lived in a corridor and the other says, "Oh, we used to dream of living in a corridor!"

Except that it was actually true in the case of my grandparents. Not the corridor. The hard life.

And I suppose that kind of thing never leaves you. I used to foster stray dogs and cats, animals that had felt true hunger. When given an unlimited supply of food, some would gorge themselves to the point of vomiting. That's survival instinct for you.

We've lost that. At least those of us who don't have to choose between buying a book or a loaf of bread have lost that.

Anyway, despite the frugal living – or rather, because of it – my grandparents were loaded financially. There was only one thing they spent real money on, and that was travel. They prioritized experiences over things and I cannot think of a wiser, more fulfilling way to live.

So really, I learned two very important life and marriage lessons from my grandparents. I hope you will indulge me as I share them with you – because honestly, they were in a minimalist marriage long before it was "a thing." And they did it right.

The first thing I learned is to **fix rather than replace**. I still have an old wooden stool that my grandpa had. If you turn it over, you can see about four screws and two metal plates, evidence that he had fixed it when it broke instead of buying a new one.

We can apply that to marriage itself, can't we? The other grass isn't always greener. Considering the problems and higher divorce rates associated with second and subsequent marriages, all else being equal, it may be better to care for the marriage we have than take our chances on another one.

The second thing I learned is to **prioritize experiences over things**, especially experiences that we share with our spouse and the people we love.

This doesn't mean you have to spend thousands and thousands of dollars to travel the world (although it's great if you can!). For a minimalist marriage to work on a day-to-day basis, we need to find value in the little experiences, the small moments.

We can take page out of my grandparents' book for that one, too. Every Sunday afternoon they took a drive together. If my sister and I were staying there, as we often did, we jumped into the backseat and away we went.

For a drive. In our own small town, the one where we knew every street sign, every house, every pot hole. My grandparents didn't listen to music much, so we just talked. Told stories. Made jokes. Got an ice-cream and then drove back home.

It's a tradition that, as old fashioned as it seems, is one that more and more modern couples are embracing. Just taking a drive together. A Sunday afternoon drive with the kids. Or a Friday night drive, as a couple, under the stars, just listening to music and talking.

Take some advice from an old school minimalist couple and just try it. Try to fix what's broken instead of replacing it. Try to prioritize experiences over things. You have nothing to lose (other than debt, anxiety, delayed retirement, clutter, etc.).

## BRIGHT IDEA #40

The word "no" is an important one to say in a minimalist marriage. "No, I'm not going to buy that" or "No, I don't need that."

And this: "No, I'm sorry we can't make it."

That last one tends to stick in the throat more, doesn't it?

When the in-laws, other family members or friends ask us to do something – *Come for supper! Spend Easter with us*! – it's hard to say no. It's so hard, in fact, that many of us say "yes" when inside we're screaming, *no!!!*

And then things get more complicated than they needed to be. We might have to change or delay our own plans, even if our plans were to do absolutely nothing.

We might have to disappoint our spouse or kids by dragging them someplace they don't really want to go. We might have to buy supplies or groceries for an event we didn't really want to host or attend. All of this just creates drama and the potential for conflict.

I don't know about you, but I've had people say "no" to me before. I've invited someone over or asked them something or other, and heard back, "Sorry, Deb, we can't do it. Too much on the go."

I lived through it.

And so will the people you want to say "no" to.

Part of a successful minimalist marriage means **minimizing the amount of people we feel obligated to say "yes" to.**

Naturally, our spouse and our kids are always our first priority and our obligation to them supersedes all others.

Yet we have obligations to other people as well, such as our employer or clients. Providing the relationships are good, we are also obligated to our parents and siblings. And then there are those few friends that are always there for us when we need them. We're obligated to them, too.

If your list is any longer than this, it's probably getting a little too long; however, the question isn't just how many people we're obligated to, it's whether those obligations – whether maintaining those relationships in a healthy way – should require us to say "yes" when we really want to say "no."

I've found that one simple way to avoid saying "yes" when we want to say "no" is to say neither. That's because we often agree to something when we're caught off-guard.

Instead, your default response to an unexpected invitation or request might be to say something like: "Thank you for the invitation (or) That sounds like fun, but I can't commit right now. I need to see what my spouse and kids have on the go."

Once you do this a few times, you'll find that the world doesn't end. And if the relationship you have with the other person is a good one, it won't end either. They will live through your "no."

Sometimes, it comes down to the lesser of two evils. Do you risk upsetting someone who has no business being upset by your "no" or do you risk upsetting your spouse and kids by your "yes"?

## Bright Idea #41

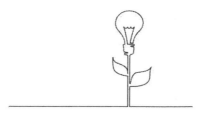

I'll let you in on a little secret. Whenever I'm faced with a very high-conflict couple in the office, a couple who has a lot of emotions and accusations flying between them, I'll turn to the most simple of all conflict resolution principles, the thing you learn on day one of any mediation class.

And that is to **find common ground.**

When we are in conflict with our spouse, we tend to focus on the differences between us and the divide between us. The more we focus on those things, the bigger the differences and the greater the divide then seem.

Luckily, the opposite is also true. When we focus on our shared interests, on the things we both want or value, the smaller the differences and the more narrow the divide. Things feel simpler. Our problems are minimized and seem more manageable.

Yet it's one thing for me – an objective party – to identify those shared interests and thus find common ground when faced with a couple in conflict or a complicated situation. Objectivity makes it easier to think. But what about you? What can you do to find common ground when you're mired in conflict and confusion?

Well, you can do the same thing.

Yes, it's true that you may be more emotional; however, it's also true that you know your spouse better than I do, better than any practitioner. You can use that knowledge to your advantage.

You know what and who your spouse loves. You know what they value and hold dear, and what they fear. You know their goals and dreams for the future. You know what kind of marriage they really want to have. You know what they want to happen.

You know all these things because you want them, too.

Shared interests are those fundamental things that connect us and that can motivate us to work through our problems in a collaborative and positive way. **These are the ties that bind.** They are the values, needs, fears and hopes that we have in common.

These are the things that initially drew you together. They are the same things that can keep you together. So use them. Identify them, talk about them, focus on them and rely on them.

Your similarities are far more powerful and useful than your differences. Use them to bring a sense of solidarity to your marriage and to the way you approach conflict. A minimalist marriage always stands on common ground. That's what makes it so stable.

## Bright Idea #42

You've heard of helicopter parents. These are the folks who hover overhead at all times, overseeing all aspects of their child's life. They're well-meaning and loving, but they're smothering.

A similar dynamic can happen in a marriage when one spouse becomes a helicopter partner.

They delegate a little too much. They monitor and micromanage. If they see their spouse sitting on the couch, even for a moment, they ask them to do something. *"Can you take out the garbage?" "Can you go online and pay the bills?"*

And that's just when they're under the same roof. Luckily for die-hard helicopter partners, personal technology makes hovering possible regardless of location.

Is your husband enjoying a rare evening of drinks with his friends or co-workers? Don't worry, you can still text him. *"Do you remember where you put the broom?" "When will you be home?"*

Has your wife managed to slip away for an afternoon shopping trip with her sister? That's okay, you can still reach her via text. *"I can't find Jake's sippy cup...do you know where it is?" "I need a new pair of shoes. Can you pick some out for me since you're at the mall?"*

Sure, things need to get done. But they don't always need to get done on our timeline. Sometimes giving our spouse the freedom to zone out and enjoy themselves can make our home life more pleasant and less cluttered with those menial tasks that never end.

Sometimes saying, "Go relax, you need a break," is more important than emptying the garbage. It shows our spouse that we respect them and appreciate all the things they do. Sometimes putting a little more effort into finding that sippy cup on our own, without texting our spouse, is the wiser option.

I promise, your spouse will notice and will love the change. And most likely, they'll start doing the same for you. Loosening up, lightening up, letting go a bit.

**A minimalist marriage strives for freedom. Freedom from financial debt, from clutter, from unnecessary conflict. But also freedom from each other to some extent.**

So resist the urge to monitor and micromanage. Resist the urge to say "Where are you going?" when your partner is clearly going downstairs. Don't talk to them through doors – it can wait a minute! Let them be.

It's important to "just be." It's healthy. People – adults and children – need time to zone out and play (see bright idea #36). Which leads me to a related point: **don't overbook yourselves or your children.**

I've seen too many couples create unnecessary drama in their marriage and family life by overbooking. There's this idea in our society that we need to have our kids in every activity: soccer, hockey, karate, dance, piano, Spanish lessons and so on. Some pre-teens have schedules that would rival the CEO of a multinational.

As a result, parents are run off their feet and kids are exhausted and moody. Yes, you need to prepare your kids for life. Good grades and life skills are important and we all want our kids to have an advantage. But balance is also important. Thinking for yourself is also important. Never mind the neighbor who has hired an Olympic swim coach for their kid and eats every meal in the car. **Live family life on your own terms.** Your kids will thank you.

## BRIGHT IDEA #43

A minimalist marriage is a question of degrees. Some people will go all the way and live off the grid, sliding solar panels onto the ceiling of their eco-home and churning their own butter.

But that's probably not you. More likely, you're looking to simply cut down on spending, clutter and conflict. Less drama, more happiness. You're rejecting abject consumerism, but those Amazon packages still come to the door now and then.

It's all good. Yet there's one element of what we might call eco-minimalism that I really want you to embrace in a way that fits your lifestyle. That's growing your own food…sort of.

Nothing tastes as good as greens and herbs plucked fresh from a garden. And when they're from your own garden, they come with a great sense of **self-sufficiency and simplicity** that perfectly complements a minimalist marriage.

You don't need to live in the country or have a big backyard in suburbia to grow your own food. If you do, great. Plant a garden, the bigger the better, and get some dirt on your knees.

But even you high-rise urbanites out there can do this. And frankly, you can do it in a way that's pretty damn cool.

Container or vertical gardens come in all shapes and sizes, and staple vegetables such as lettuce, carrots and tomatoes can be grown either on your balcony or indoors (yep, right in your kitchen) with great success.

Just think how much fun your kids will have stopping at the wall-garden on their way to the table to pluck some fresh lettuce or pull a sweet carrot from the soil. It's a fun thing to do. And hey, company will think you're super chic.

If even this seems like too much of a horticultural commitment to you, don't worry. It gets even easier.

Hydroponic indoor gardens can grow a variety of vegetables and herbs, and all without getting your hands dirty. Many of these serve double-duty as garden and décor – they're stylish, beautifully fragrant, and add vibrant color to any room.

You can even put hydroponic pots and gardens in multiple rooms: the kitchen, the study, the living room. We know a couple who has several of them. We call their apartment the *Enterprise*. At meal-time, we just snip off a little of this or that herb and add it to our dish.

Again, there is just something very natural and empowering about growing your own food, even if it's just a pot of herbs. Even the simple act of snipping off a bit of basil or cilantro from your own hydroponic garden instead of buying it from the store in a freeze-dried jar can make a difference.

## BRIGHT IDEA #44

Remember how I bored the life out of you back in bright idea #27 when I spoke about reliability? Well, get ready for another heart-pounding entry. What can I say, I'm an adrenaline junkie. This bright idea is about…wait for it…*taking care of yourself.*

Or more specifically, taking care of yourself – body and mind – in simple, common sense, even economical ways. Because those are the only ways that work.

Whenever I speak about this, I think of a certain client. He was a former professional hockey player but after retirement he had gained a lot of weight and it was really bringing him down.

It was also affecting his marriage. The extra weight was adding extra self-consciousness that was manifesting as anger. And that in turn was causing a host of problems between he and his wife.

Anyway, after years spent immersed in the kind of supervised high-tech diet and fitness regime that professional athletes have, this particular gentleman was having trouble going it alone.

In an effort to take off the extra weight, and despite admitting that he should've known better, he nonetheless fell into the trap of trying different "fads." He tried all kinds of supplements, magic weight loss pills, extreme nutritional changes or food eliminations and so on. He bought expensive low-fat grills, food processors and an elaborate juicer.

In fact, it was the juicer that, according to his wife, was the straw that broke the camel's back. Three times a day she'd find it piled into the sink, its multiple inner parts packed with fruit bits. Juice, pulp, seeds and peelings were spread over the counter to leave sticky patches everywhere.

She was tired of cleaning it. She was tired of her husband's attitude. The whole thing was becoming a lot more complicated than it needed to be.

The good news was that my client was a fast learner. After an initial consult he realized where his anger was coming from and his marriage started to improve. He also turned to a very good dietician who told him – guess what? – simple is better. Complex fads and eating habits just don't work.

Taking care of yourself, body and mind, shouldn't be a complicated endeavor. The truth is, **simple is sustainable.** And that's true of so many things in this book, isn't it? That's what a minimalist marriage is about.

I've seen health issues impact marriages in all kinds of ways. Remember when I used the whack-a-mole analogy (see bright idea #12) to discuss the effect of debt? It's a similar situation with health problems, specifically the ones that are self-inflicted.

When we don't take care of ourselves, when we neglect or abuse our own bodies, we create a host of offshoot problems and complications that would not have otherwise existed.

The healthier spouse may worry about their unhealthier counterpart, but they may also be frustrated with them, too. They might miss doing more activities. They might miss intimacy.

The unhealthier spouse may resent their healthier counterpart's energy level or attitude. They may feel insecure and hopeless, and that can really bring down the mood in a marriage.

Hey, the clock's ticking for all of us. We're all getting older, we're all facing the reality that our bodies will ultimately fail us. We'll all lose our mobility and independence at some point.

Sorry to get all heavy on you but, to misquote Shakespeare, we all owe the universe a death. But honestly, we don't need to jump ahead, do we? We don't need to pay up early.

Unnecessary medical issues, the kind we bring about ourselves by not taking care of our body and mind, can needlessly complicate our life and our marriage in the worst way possible.

So keep it simple. Eat well. Eat fresh. Eat a variety of foods and practice portion control. Move your body.

You don't need to clutter your cupboards with sketchy diet pills. You don't need to clutter your counters with expensive juicers. In fact, I've heard many couples lament the amount of money they wasted on such things.

Whenever they saw that juicer just sitting there taking up space, they weren't just reminded of the money they wasted on it. They were also reminded of the failed diet attempt.

So keep it simple. Simplicity is sustainable. Simplicity leads to success. Simplicity can prevent complications, both in terms of health and in terms of your marriage.

## BRIGHT IDEA #45

There's an old joke that I'm going to tell all wrong, but here it goes anyway.

A man walks into pub, orders a drink at the bar and strikes up a conversation with the guy sitting next to him.

After a short time, a woman walks into the pub and the guy says, "Hey, check out that woman. She's beautiful."

The man responds, "That's not a woman. That's my wife."

Get it?

When we're with our spouse for a long time, it's easy to take them for granted. We stop seeing them as a real person and we starting seeing them as "just" our husband or wife.

And that's where the problems start. All kinds of problems.

On the less serious end of the spectrum, we let our manners and compliments slip. We forget to do (or don't bother to do) all the "little things" anymore.

We stop meeting our spouse at the door. Our voice tone becomes less affectionate. We become more impatient.

On the more serious end of the spectrum, we disrespect them. We break our promises and betray their trust. We break their heart.

There are a thousand reasons why spouses fall out of love, but there is one reason above all: we start taking each other for granted. We stop seeing each other as an actual person!

I see this play out in marriages all the time. It's almost always an underlying theme of affairs and inappropriate friendships. Too often, a person begins to think less of their spouse and more of someone else, including themselves (see bright idea #15).

It's only when the marriage itself is at risk that this person realizes the hard truth: their spouse *is* a real person. And divorce is a real possibility.

In any case, as with so many other things, a word to the wise is sufficient. **Remember that your spouse isn't just your husband or wife, they're a real person.**

When you're out in public, try to see your spouse the way other people do: as interesting, appealing, attractive. If you see someone steal a glance at your spouse, use that little bit of jealousy as a friendly reminder that someone else out there wouldn't take them for granted. And you shouldn't either.

If you can remember this simple bit of advice, your life and your marriage will have a lot less drama and a lot more happiness. And that's the whole reason you want a minimalist marriage, isn't it?

## BRIGHT IDEA #46

Picture me sitting in my office. Across from me sits a well-dressed, middle-aged man with his hands on the armrests of his chair. He looks uncomfortable. Worried. But also very surprised.

"I never thought she'd leave me," he says.

"Did she tell you she was unhappy?" I ask.

"No, never."

"Did she ever express any kind of complaints?"

"Well, she always complains that I don't help around the house or do much with the kids. But she never said she's *unhappy*."

Yes, this was a real conversation. In fact, I've had more of these conversations than I can remember.

If you want to avoid unnecessary conflict and complications in your life, if want to have a minimalist marriage that is low on drama and high on happiness, tattoo this on your heart: **always take your spouse's complaints seriously.**

Too often, a spouse will brush off a partner's complaints as unfounded or unimportant. They might downplay their partner's complaints or even tell their partner that they're wrong to express them. They might get angry and just counter with their own complaints.

And then when things reach their breaking point, they act surprised. They might actually blame their partner for not expressing the complaint in a different or more specific way.

**Well, sometimes in marriage you need to read between the lines.** If your partner doesn't seem happy, if they've expressed some kind of complaint or dissatisfaction – even quietly, even in passing – please, take it seriously!

Don't dismiss them or get defensive. Don't steamroll over them with your own complaints.

Just listen. Listen like you care. Acknowledge their feelings and your own shortcomings, and commit to doing better.

Don't make it more complicated than this. Don't add clutter.

This approach is the best, easiest, fastest and lowest-conflict way to stop conflict and drama before it starts. There is no downside to it. It is risk-free.

It is also the best, easiest, fastest and lowest-conflict way to prompt your spouse to take your complaints seriously. That's because "like attracts like" in marriage (see bright idea #7). This simple philosophy should be found in every minimalist marriage.

## BRIGHT IDEA #47

Many years ago, I visited – of all places – a legal brothel in Nevada. Now before you make any assumptions about that, it was for a pending book deal. One of the women who worked there had some publicity come her way and I was asked to ghost-write a book about her experience. Long story short, the book deal fell through, as they often do, but it was nonetheless an eye-opening experience for me. And probably not for the reasons you think.

What surprised me most about the place was how relaxed and welcoming it was. And that was all by design. Rich colors, high-end furniture, low lighting, soft carpets, music playing in the background, the works.

The women who worked there were kind enough to give me a tour of the place, and the thing that really struck me was their bedrooms. Each woman decorated her own room, yet they all had a few similarities.

They were painted with bold, deep colors of red or blue or green. They boasted heavy velvet drapes. There were lots of differently colored and differently textured cushions on the bed. Many of the beds had canopies or those mesh mosquito nets that envelope the whole bed.

Most of the rooms were lit by candles or some kind of muted color lamp. Fragrance, perhaps incense or some kind of aromatherapy oils or candles, was pleasantly noticeable.

The moment you crossed the threshold into one of these luxurious bedrooms, you knew exactly what was supposed to happen in there. The ambience was about as sensual as it gets – I mean sensual in a literal way – what you saw, what you smelled, the physical sensation of the space...it really made an impact.

And that's something that a lot of our bedrooms *don't* do nowadays. These days, many of our bedrooms are fairly bland. White, beige or grey walls. Nice but not all that interesting art on the walls. Linen that's just okay. Vertical blinds instead of drapes. A bedside lamp with a glaring white bulb and the power cord for our phone twisted around the base.

I really think we need to do better. Think about it – your bedroom is the one place on the planet that you and your spouse have entirely to yourselves.

Nobody else really needs to go in there. Sure, if you have kids at home and they're sick or have a bad dream, then of course they're going to pile in the bed with you. But all else being equal, it really is a private space for you and your spouse.

A couple's bedroom should be a sensual sanctuary. A retreat, an escape from the world where you can reconnect.

When I was at that brothel I interviewed quite a few male customers and they all said the same thing. That part of the reason they chose this place, was because it was an escape. It was their time to disconnect from the obligations or stresses of their life and just bask in the sensuality of it all.

The world's a busy place, isn't it? It's loud, it's crowded, it's hectic. It's hard to carve out a peaceful or private moment. Yet peace and privacy are fundamental to a minimalist marriage, so it has to happen. It has to be a priority.

**Every couple should have a hideaway in their home: and that space should be the bedroom.** It should be your private retreat from the world.

Keep your bedroom clean and uncluttered; however, this may be the one area of your home where it's okay to splurge a little…to splurge on sensuality, at least. That can help keep the emotional and physical intimacy of your marriage alive.

There is an idea that a minimalist marriage translates to plain walls, Spartan furnishings and austere surroundings. If that's your style, great. If it isn't your style, that's okay, too. Having a minimalist marriage isn't about what's on the walls or not on the walls. It's about what's within them.

Find your own way to make your bedroom a more impactful space. If you prefer white walls over blue, vertical blinds over velvet drapes, so be it. It doesn't matter. The point is to create a sensual sanctuary and a private retreat where you don't just make your spouse feel desired (see bright idea #17), you also make them feel like they don't want to leave.

## BRIGHT IDEA #48

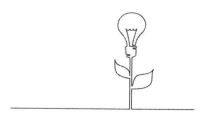

You've pocketed some great strategies to keep conflict from needlessly complicating and cluttering your minimalist marriage: put your partner first (see bright idea #7), be your partner's advocate (see bright idea #8), find common ground (see bright idea #41) and take your partner's complaints seriously (see bright idea #46).

Now, I'd like you to tuck this handy "Do and Don't" pair into your pocket as well. *Do* take a detour. *Don't* say the "d" word.

I'll elaborate.

**Do take a detour.** Many couples who find themselves having too many arguments will say there's a predictable pattern to it all. They have the same argument, at the same time, often using the same words. They always end up traveling down that same road that leads to some kind of bickering or fight, some kind of dead-end.

But think about it: if you're in your car and you know that a certain road leads to a dead-end, do you stay on it? No. You stop and change course. That's how I want you to handle these pointless, dead-end arguments that you know are just waiting for you.

If you find yourself traveling down that same road that leads to some kind of bickering or fight, to some kind of dead-end, then change course. Immediately. Stop whatever you're doing or saying and start doing and saying something different. Take a sharp detour.

The idea is to stop the cycle, to break the habit, to take a different path. Any path that doesn't lead to the same dead-end.

You can surprise your spouse with a kiss or an embrace. You can suggest that you go for a drive and get a milkshake. You can ask for a time-out and watch a cat video or a fail video online.

Just do something different, unexpected and positive. Take a detour. Remember, you don't have to solve your problem that moment (see bright idea #23). You're on a long journey together. So act like it.

**Don't say the "d" word.** Okay, this one is really a pet peeve of mine. It's when one spouse adds needless and immature drama to a situation or argument by using the "d" word – divorce.

"Maybe we should just get divorced!"

"Oh, so you want a divorce?"

A person might resort to the "d" word for any number of reasons. Perhaps they're looking for reassurance that their partner doesn't want a divorce. Or perhaps they feel unheard by their spouse and are hoping the threat will show their partner just how serious or hurt they really are. In such cases, the intent isn't evil or sinister. But it still won't help matters.

In more worrisome cases, a spouse might be trying to intimidate or control their partner. An example might be a person who is having an affair. "If you pressure me to end it, I think we should talk about getting a divorce." Or something like that. The purpose of the "d" word is to get their spouse to back down.

Whatever the reason, threatening divorce usually takes an argument or a situation to a whole new level of anxiety and worst-case imaginings full of lawyers, custody battles and asset division. It adds clutter and drama. So don't do it.

So again, tuck this "Do and Don't" pair away and keep them in mind no matter what situations or conflicts arise.

## Bright Idea #49

I've said before that minimalist marriages distill larger concepts down to their simplest form. It's what I've tried to do in this book, too.

Take the field of Aristotelian ethics. A major element of this is the ancient Greek philosopher's emphasis on practical virtue.

Now take the study of cognitive behavioral therapy. This is a complex modern psychosocial intervention used by therapists.

If I were to distill these things down – and I'm about to – this is what I'd say: **Fake it 'til you make it.**

Yes, I'm oversimplifying. Obviously. But what I've said isn't entirely untrue. Both of these areas of thought and study are focused on changing behavior for the better. Both do have a fundamental "fake it 'til you make it" element to them.

And if it's good enough for Aristotle, it's good enough for us. Fake it 'til you make it. There is a lot of wisdom in that simple statement and you should use it in your minimalist marriage.

Marriages, especially long-term marriages, go through many ups and downs. We fall in and out of love…or more accurately, we fall in and out of the *feeling* of being in love. We get irritated. We have bad days. We have days where we just don't care. We have days when someone else might be on our mind.

Through it all, through the changing emotions and wandering thoughts, one thing can keep us from making a big mistake.

Deciding to fake it 'til we make it.

This is when we decide (or force ourselves) to say, "I love you," when we don't really feel it. When we let something slide when we're annoyed. When we choose to walk into the house with a smile and not let a bad day ruin our whole evening with our family.

It's when we act like we care when we don't. When we force thoughts of that new co-worker's flirtatious grin out of our mind and instead greet our spouse with an extra long hug at the door.

Because there's no doubt that our behavior can influence our thoughts and our emotions and take us where we want to go. Behavior can lead the way.

But you already know that, don't you?

You've forced your grumpy self to smile at someone and then you started to feel happier yourself. Maybe it all came from within. Or maybe your smile prompted the other person to smile back, which in turn made you happier. It's like the old song, "When you're smiling, the whole world smiles with you."

It doesn't really matter how it works. It's enough to know that it does. And as often as not, this simple concept is enough to get you through those ups and downs, those in and outs of love, those bad moods and those passing thoughts of other people. It's enough to get you back where you want to be – with your spouse, for real.

So fake it 'til you make it. And you will make it.

## BRIGHT IDEA #50

When you think about it, a minimalist marriage is about preparing for the future: your financial future, your future well-being and the future of your marriage.

If you have kids, you're also preparing them for their future. Having a minimalist marriage and lifestyle teaches them, by example, some important lessons: how to avoid debt and how to prevent relationships and life from getting too dramatic or cluttered. You're teaching them how to be happy and you're doing that by being happy yourself. There is no downside to a minimalist marriage. Not for you, not for your children, not for the planet.

Perhaps minimalism is the next step in our sociocultural evolution. Perhaps we're finally reaching that point where we realize that less is more and we're ready to start living that.

There is something futuristic about the minimalist movement, isn't there? One of the suggestions in this book was to have an indoor hydroponic garden in your home (see bright idea #43). Not so long ago, that was pure science fiction.

Indeed, whenever I think of clutter, a certain word from world of sci-fi comes to mind – *kipple*. It comes from a science fiction novel called *Do Androids Dream of Electric Sheep* by Philip K. Dick. The movie *Blade Runner* was (loosely) based on it. The book is set in a dystopian future where everyone who has the means has left the poisoned garbage world that Earth has become.

The character Isadore says:

*Kipple is useless objects, like junk mail or match folders after you use the last match or gum wrappers or yesterday's homeopape. When nobody's around, kipple reproduces itself. For instance, if you go to bed leaving any kipple around your apartment, when you wake up the next morning there's twice as much of it. It always gets more and more.*

The character struggles to control and reduce the "kipple factor" in a world where junk begets more junk, clutter begets more clutter. All is entropy and disorder. The end of the world isn't a wasteland, it's a junkyard.

But the kipple, the clutter, isn't just physical. It represents the clutter in the lives of the characters, too. This is a world where people becoming living kipple.

If science fiction predicts the future – and it does – then we've been warned, haven't we? I've felt the connection between physical clutter on one hand and mental and emotional clutter on the other. It's the refuse that piles up first in our physical space, and then in our mental and emotional space.

So look into your future. Do you own stuff or does your stuff own you?

In this book, I've discussed reducing unnecessary and debt-incurring large purchases, such as homes and cars. I've discussed reducing household items that you don't need.

But there's another type of physical clutter – the real junk. The absolutely useless stuff. The stuff that tumbles out when you open a closet: that broken heating pad, the busted knock-off lightsaber your kid won at the fair, the decade-old bottle of glue.

It's the chaos inside your kitchen junk drawer. The stuff that doesn't even qualify as an "item," it's just pure trash. Empty tape dispensers. Wrappers. That plastic fork with the broken tine.

It's the junk that makes you feel overwhelmed when you see it, so that you just close the drawer. It's just too much. It just seems to multiply in there! Why get started, it's pointless.

You know that's not true.

Grab a garbage bag and start filling it up with trash. Don't think about it, just down a cup of strong coffee and do it.

Throw away the scratched sunglasses or broken cups. The trinkets you can't stand. The worn-down nail file. The measuring tape that doesn't roll back up anymore. The cracked picture frame. The movie ticket stubs.

Start with the real junk, the stuff you know is pure trash. Start somewhere! Once you start, you'll see that it is possible and it feels great.

Your efforts will gain momentum and you'll feel more empowered, more inspired and more liberated. It will get easier and easier to have a minimalist lifestyle.

Have a clear, uncluttered vision of the future you want for yourself and your spouse. Walk boldly toward it, metaphorical trash bag in hand, and get to work. Get rid of what you don't want. It's the only way to make room for what you do want.

# GOODBYE

My purpose in this book has been to give you simple, bare minimum strategies that you can remember to both avoid and resolve conflict in your minimalist marriage. Such strategies have to be simple. If they aren't, we forget them in the heat of the moment and the situation becomes cluttered with more problems and more drama.

I've gathered some of these strategies from larger concepts and adapted them from my training in communication, law, mediation and conflict resolution. But I've also chosen them for this book because I've seen them work in the real world, for real clients. I sincerely hope they work for you, too.

Yet this book isn't just about preventing or solving problems. It's also about encouraging you, as a couple, to challenge the ways that society expects you to spend your hard-earned money, as well as your valuable time and precious energy.

It's about de-cluttering not just your space, but also your mind and emotions. It's about recognizing what is important, having a conscious marriage and living life on your own terms. If you're reading this book, you're already the type of person that tends to do that. So keep doing it.

Thank you for reading.

All the best,
Debra Macleod

## About the Author

Debra Macleod, B.A., LL.B., is an international marriage author and conflict specialist who offers a no-nonsense, innovative alternative to couples counseling. Her books have been translated into several languages and her marriage-saving programs have helped countless couples get over their problems and get on with life.

You can visit her at DebraMacleod.com.

Made in the USA
Lexington, KY
05 September 2019